SEEKING JESUS OF NAZARETH

*This book is dedicated to
students, past and present*

Maurice Hogan SSC

Seeking Jesus of Nazareth

AN INTRODUCTION TO THE CHRISTOLOGY
OF THE FOUR GOSPELS

the columba press

First published in 2001 by
the columba press
55A Spruce Avenue, Stillorgan Industrial Park,
Blackrock, Co Dublin

Cover by Bill Bolger
Origination by The Columba Press
Printed in Ireland by Colour Books Ltd, Dublin

ISBN 1 85607 331 9

Contents

Prologue

The last two decades or so have witnessed a proliferation of books on Jesus flooding the market and this has attracted an enormous interest on the part of the media. Some time ago, a few influential and widely read weekly magazines pictured Jesus on their covers. On the surface, such publicity ought to be warmly welcomed by the churches with their diminishing congregations. However, this is hardly the case. These publications often portray the Jesus the researchers wished to find, and are reminiscent of the nineteenth century liberal quest for the historical Jesus. Sensational headlines in newspapers serve only to create confusion in the minds of many Christians as to who the real Jesus is, and sow seeds of doubt regarding the reliability of the gospels themselves to tell us anything about him. Much of the media interest generated by recent books rests on the claim that historical investigation can challenge Christians' faith in Jesus. It assumes that the 'real' Jesus is different from the one worshipped by believers.

For Christians, however, the significance of Jesus is determined, not by the latest novelty, nor by sources outside of Christianity, but by the death and resurrection of Jesus. As risen Lord, Jesus is alive in the community he founded and in the lives of Christians. This is the real Jesus. The gospels can be relied on to provide access to the real Jesus and a true appreciation of him precisely insofar as they reflect the perception of him given by his post-resurrection existence. For this reason an attitude of suspicion needs to be replaced by an attitude of trust. Although Christianity does have an historical dimension, and historians can offer important assertions about Jesus' person and ministry, as we shall see, these are naturally limited in scope.

While a full biography of Jesus in the modern sense is hardly attainable, the gospel portraits of Jesus, especially the Lukan, do have features in common with ancient biographies or 'Lives' of famous people. What is attainable though, is a faith interpretation of Jesus' life and ministry given in the gospels. This book is written to assist the reader in understanding and appreciating the Jesus that is portrayed in the four gospels. Far from being a substitute for reading the gospels themselves, it is best read alongside them. The reader should first read through the complete text of the gospels, or at least an individual gospel, before reading the chapter devoted to its christology. To facilitate this reading, an outline of the individual gospels is given together with the storyline, to help readers who may be unfamiliar with the narrative's overall content and features. Having read the relevant chapter, it is suggested that the gospel narrative be read again slowly and meditatively.[1] This method is born out of the self-evident notion that each of the gospels constitutes a unified narrative whose individual parts cannot be read in isolation without violating the gospel narrative itself. This also has implications for the christology of each of the gospels. Why? Because the christology is in the narrative itself – what Jesus says and does, how he relates and what he undergoes – as well as in the titles that pertain to him. Although the evangelists incorporated sources both oral and written in composing their narratives it is, nevertheless, in their final composition that the portrait of Jesus, peculiar to each, emerges.

This book is an introduction to the way Jesus is understood in the gospels and should serve as a useful aid for students and those interested in learning about Jesus, the Son of the living God, as set out in the gospels. It should also be of help to believing Christians who may be confused by the popularisation of scholarly views and critical discussion. We shall limit ourselves to what is generally agreed among mainline scholars who are

1. Such meditative reading provided important nourishment for the spiritual life in medieval times. It was called *lectio divina* or spiritual reading, and is still a most valuable way to engage the gospels.

writing today. An introductory chapter will consider matters pertinent to the proper appreciation of the gospel writings: the centrality of the resurrection experience, the development of christology, as well as the nature of the gospel writings themselves. A chapter will be devoted to each of the gospels in turn, giving an outline and storyline before examining its christological portrait. A further chapter will discuss what can be known about the historical Jesus, and a concluding chapter will show that despite their diversity, the gospels do show a remarkable consistency in their portraits of Jesus. A select bibliography for further reading is offered at the end of the book.

My indebtedness to many contemporary scholars is gratefully acknowledged. A special word of thanks is due to my colleagues, past and present, in the scripture department at Maynooth College and to Caroline Nolan, a student at the Biblicum, for their helpful suggestions and encouragement; to Rev Seamus Doyle, pastor of St Rose of Lima Church, Miami, and the rector, staff and students of the Irish College, Rome, for their hospitality during the writing of this book.

CHAPTER ONE

Approaching the Gospel Narratives

THE CENTRALITY OF THE RESURRECTION EXPERIENCE

At the centre of Christianity is the resurrection experience. It all began with the followers of Jesus experiencing Jesus after his death in an entirely new way. That 'resurrection faith' is at the birth of Christianity. It is already evident from the earliest Christian writings in the middle of the first century (cf. 1 Thess 1:9-10). In 1 Cor 15:3-8, Paul refers to a tradition he himself had received before he evangelised the Corinthians. In this formula the belief in the saving power of Jesus' death, his resurrection and the post-Easter appearances go back to the very beginning of the church's existence. The death of Jesus on the cross fulfilled God's salvific plan 'according to the scriptures'. The raising of Jesus follows on his death and burial and reverses them. What Paul relates is the experiential basis of the good news. Christ was raised from the dead and was experienced by many people, including Paul himself. They did not encounter a Jesus who was still living in the ordinary way, but experienced him as risen Lord. Over five hundred people, Paul tells us, had the same experience, many of whom were still alive at the time of writing.

In the first century of the Christian era there was an expectation in Judaism of victory over death that was linked with the eschatological world which the just will inherit once death has been definitively vanquished (cf. Dan 12:1-3; 2 Macc 7:9, 14, 23; Wis 3:1-9). The early preaching applied this expectation to the resurrection of Jesus. The new age has dawned because Jesus of Nazareth has been raised from the dead, 'the first-fruits of those who have fallen asleep' (1 Cor 15:20). Just as the first sheaf represents the entire harvest, so also those who belong to Christ will share in his victory over death.

The New Testament does not say that anyone actually saw the resurrection, nor does it make any attempt to describe it. The reality of the resurrection is based on two facts: the missing body or empty tomb, and the validity of the experiences of those who claim to have seen the risen Christ. The empty tomb provides the background for the Easter stories in the gospels. The disciples who preached the risen Christ did so because they knew that the tomb was empty. Their preaching would have been quickly discredited if Jesus' body still lay in the tomb. Since their opponents never insinuated that the tomb was not empty, this suggests continuity between the Jesus of the earthly life and the transformed Jesus who appeared to the disciples.

In the gospels there are narratives that tell us about some of these experiences which stem from eyewitness accounts, although now shaped to bring them into line with the literary and religious purposes of each of the gospels. There is first of all the empty tomb accounts (Mk 16:1-8; Mt 20:1-8; Lk 24:1-11; Jn 20:1-10) that tell of the followers of Jesus coming to the tomb to anoint the body of Jesus after his death, only to discover that the body was not there. They are told by heavenly messengers to tell the disciples that he has been raised. Jesus is absent from the place of death, he is not where he was buried. The linens left behind bear witness to one who has been freed from death (cf Jn 20:6-9). The empty tomb leaves open the possibility of new encounters with Jesus.

The second type of resurrection narrative found in the gospels is the appearance accounts (Mk 16:9-20; Mt 28:9-10, 16-20; Lk 24:13-49; Jn 20:11-29; 21:1-23). They are isolated appearances so a sequence cannot be established. In time they became attached to two locations, Jerusalem and Galilee, but neither shows any awareness of the other. Each tradition centres on an appearance in which disciples are commissioned for a future mission. Christian communities in Galilee and Jerusalem would have remembered appearances with local associations. What was important, though, was not the time or location, but the testimony of well-known witnesses who had seen Jesus.

Some of the narrative accounts stress the reality of Jesus' resurrected body to make it clear that the one who now lives is identified with the one who died, and that the experience of his presence is not that of a ghost or phantom (cf Jn 20:26-28; Lk 24:36-43). The narratives also reveal the suddenness of these encounters that were both surprising and unexpected. Jesus appears unrecognised to two disciples on the road to Emmaus; Mary Magdalene initially mistakes him for the gardener; he appears suddenly through locked doors, and he ascends into heaven. The narratives express both continuity and discontinuity. The same Jesus is present in an entirely new way, in a transformed, glorified body.

But above all these narratives are dominated by the words spoken by Jesus who interprets the scriptures for the disciples and commands them to go out and preach the message to others. The powerful experience of the risen Lord leads to the proclamation of the good news. Nevertheless, the experience of the risen Lord is not confined to these narratives. He continues to be present in a personal, transcendent and transforming manner within the Christian community; in the eucharistic Bread, in the forgiveness of sins, in the Christian interpretation of the scriptures, and in the preaching and mission of the church (cf Lk 24:13-48). In the early chapters of Acts, the experience of power is associated with the outpouring of the Holy Spirit (cf Acts 2:32-33), enabling the disciples to confess and proclaim their faith. This Holy Spirit is the life-giving presence of the risen Lord. The conviction that Jesus is alive and powerfully active through his Spirit in the believing community underlies all the New Testament writings, including the gospels. Jesus is not simply a figure of the past, nostalgically remembered. He is the living Lord whose words continue to address believers in the present.

The resurrection faith that gave birth to the Christian movement created the need for interpretation as well as proclamation. It was not enough for the first Christians to experience the transforming power of the Spirit and proclaim Jesus as Lord. They also had to interpret their lives in the light of them. This interpretation inevitably centered on the person of Jesus. The risen Lord who had appeared to the disciples was identified with the same Jesus who had been put to death on the cross, who had preached, taught and worked miracles in their midst. Their memories of the earthly Jesus were shaped by preaching, teaching, worship and social contexts that contributed to the finished literary products we call 'gospels'. Such were the generative experiences that gave rise to the Christian movement. They show the need both to remember Jesus and the shape the narratives took. We will now glance at how the content of the gospels came to be, before looking at the nature of sources, the gospel narratives, and the stages in their formation.

THE SHAPING OF GOSPEL CHRISTOLOGY

Introduction

To what extent did the early Christians' and evangelists' preaching and writing about Jesus actually correspond to the image of Jesus reflected in what he said and did? Was Jesus more than an ordinary human being? Is the christology we find in the gospels an erroneous view that does not stand in real continuity with Jesus' own self-understanding? It appears that many scholars now accept that the portraits of Jesus we find in the four gospels are grounded on who Jesus actually was, what he said and what he did, what happened to him during his earthly life and ministry and his suffering and death on the cross. Jesus was no ordinary first-century Palestinian Jew whom the church later dressed up to give the newly fledged Christian movement a modicum of credibility. This does not mean, though, that there was no growth or development in the church's understanding of the person of Jesus and his significance during the first century of our era, a development that is reflected in the gospel christologies themselves. There is however, no non-christological Jesus to be uncovered. The earthly Jesus was no mere Palestinian peasant or wandering philosopher!

Christology involves more than assessing the titles applied to Jesus, although these have their place in the discussion that follows.

It is also concerned with the person, ministry, relationships and experiences of Jesus. As well as these, it seems that either Jesus himself or the early church, or possibly both, changed or modified some current Jewish understandings of Messiah, Son of God, Son of Man, and others, by infusing new meanings into old symbols. This was all the more necessary since a crucified Messiah called for some explanation because it was something contemporary Jews were not expecting. Some of these changes were brought about as a result of re-reading the Old Testament in the light of the life and ministry of Jesus, and not just his death on the cross.

Before turning to the christologies of the gospels, we will have to look at contemporary Jewish expectations, Jesus' self-understanding and self-presentation, as well as the period between the death of Jesus and the composition of the gospels themselves. This will lend an opportunity of seeing how the gospel christologies unfolded and developed. It took time for the full significance of Jesus to be appreciated by the early church after the resurrection experiences, and to find the right words, concepts and symbols that were deemed suitable to convey a sense of the person and work of Jesus. The application of old terms to Jesus was not enough. The events of his life, especially his suffering, death and resurrection led to a creative re-reading and re-interpretation of the Old Testament. What we find in the gospels, then, is the history of Jesus of Nazareth related to various Old Testament texts and symbols in order to explain and interpret the facts about his life.

Jewish Expectations

By the first century of our era there was a variety of expectations among the Jews. A consideration of these will serve as background to both assessing Jesus' self-understanding and the gospel christologies.

Jewish expectation of a Messiah began to emerge in the post-exilic period when the Davidic kings ceased to rule. The longing for an ideal king who would save his people shifted to the indef-

inite future. The prophecies and royal psalms were re-read with
this understanding in mind. In Zech 9:9ff, for example, all the
trappings of power disappear, yet the Messiah's reign will bring
universal peace. In the centuries immediately preceding the
Christian era, there was the expectation of a political Messiah.
The Jews not only longed for spiritual renewal, they also wanted
their nation freed from foreign domination. Since a suffering
Messiah did not have a place in their thinking, this title had to
undergo considerable modification before it could be applied to
Jesus. The Christian understanding of a Messiah whose kingdom was not of this world also represented a significant change,
hence Jesus' apparent reluctance to accept the title without qualification. It took time for Jewish expectations to be altered in the
light of Jesus' total career, so that the Christian could acknowledge him as Messiah in all phases of his life.

Some groups like the Qumran community interpreted various Old Testament texts messianically and eschatologically. Yet,
no Jewish literature of the time attests to a 'divine status' for the
expected Messiah, so it is noteworthy that Jesus was the only
historical person to be identified with the Son of Man in Daniel
7:13. There the figure of someone 'like a son of man' appears in
the clouds of heaven to receive power and authority from God.
Later reflection in apocalyptic circles (1 Enoch, IV Ezra) gave rise
to a messianic human figure of heavenly origin who is glorified
by God and appointed judge. Against this background, Jesus
could have used this terminology in his self-presentation.

Another Old Testament strand that stands out in the background was the notion of God's Wisdom, the personification of
a divine attribute. Already present in Proverbs (ch 8), it is prominent in the later books of Sirach (ch 24), Baruch (ch 3-4) and
Wisdom of Solomon (ch 7-9). Wisdom is described as having its
origin in God, it pre-existed creation and had a role in it. It
comes into the world to offer life, prosperity and blessings to
those who follow its ways. Wisdom was associated with Israel,
was at work in its history, and was partially identified with the
Torah because it expressed God's revelation. In later literature (1

Enoch), Wisdom finds no permanent dwelling on earth and returns to heaven.

Jesus' Self-Presentation

No lesser authority on christology than J. D. G. Dunn believes that in the synoptic tradition we have direct access to the teaching and ministry of Jesus, as it was actually remembered by those who accompanied him during his ministry.

> Through the main body of the synoptic tradition, I believe, we have in most cases direct access to the teaching and ministry of Jesus as it was remembered from the beginning in the transmission process (which often predates Easter), and also fairly direct access to the ministry and teaching of Jesus through the eyes and ears of those who went about with him. [2]

Those who handed on the Jesus traditions were more preservers than innovators, who sought to transmit and re-tell, as well as explain and interpret, but they did not create or 'make it all up'. It appears that Jesus had an exalted self-understanding and this will become evident when we consider the gospel material. In the gospels there is first of all indirect evidence stemming from Jesus' relationships with individuals and groups, as well as what he did and the experiences he had. There is evidence of a more direct nature in the titles Jesus used concerning himself. Both indirect and direct evidence suggests that Jesus viewed himself in a christological light.[3]

If, as the synoptics reveal, Jesus viewed John the Baptist as the last great eschatological prophet, indeed as more than a prophet (cf Mt 11:7-11; Lk 7:24-28), then by implication this also tells us something about how Jesus viewed himself. Furthermore, regarding Jesus' confrontations with the Pharisees as related in the gospels, it is less than convincing to say that these are

2. J. D. G. Dunn, 'Messianic Ideas and Their Influence on the Jesus of History', (1992) in *The Christ and the Spirit: Volume I Christology*, Grand Rapids: Eerdmans, 1998, p. 85

3. Cf Ben Witherington III, *The Christology of Jesus*, Philadelphia: Fortress Press, 1990, pp 33-143

purely a result of ongoing disagreements between church and synagogue in the post-Easter period. A more plausible explanation is that Jesus did engage in heated controversies with the Pharisees of his day. This surely tells us something about his self-understanding. Either Jesus was a law-breaking Jew when he healed on the Sabbath and ate with ritually unclean and immoral people, or else he assumed an authority over both the oral and written Law that the Pharisees refused to recognise (cf Mk 7:5-16). Jesus never cited Jewish authorities for his teaching. He taught with authority as if he had a right to speak for God ('Amen, I say to you...'). There was no hint that, unlike the Old Testament prophets, the word of the Lord came to him; he seemed clearly to possess it. As Jesus said, he had come to inaugurate the definitive reign of God (cf Mk 1:15). It seems then that Jesus stood apart from the Pharisees and would have been seen as a threat to their teaching. He felt free to cast aside what had long been recognised as having sacred status. All of this points to someone with a very exalted sense of his own authority, one who interpreted the Mosaic Law and must have had divine authorisation to do so. His authority to make demands in God's name resided in Jesus simply because of who he was. Jesus claimed to be greater than Old Testament figures, and this implies a special relationship with the God of Israel.

Jesus had a close relationship with his followers, in particular with the inner circle of the Twelve who symbolised the twelve tribes of Israel. He sent them out to the lost sheep of Israel to invite repentance in view of the in-breaking of God's reign. This suggests that Jesus saw himself as some kind of shepherd or leader, even God's special agent (cf Mt 10:40). Indeed, this is scarcely the attitude of an ordinary teacher or leader. Jesus had an exalted view of his mission and message as one who was to inaugurate the imminent reign of God. This is the impression that comes from the cumulative effect of a variety of different traditions within the gospels. It is unthinkable that all of them would have been created by the early church. A more credible explanation is that they do in fact go back to the ministry of Jesus himself.

Further evidence to support this view is found in what Jesus did. The miracles of Jesus are as old as his words; they are found in all the gospel traditions and therefore must be taken seriously. The miracles, healings and exorcisms are all intimately related to his teaching as works of power associated with the reign of God. Even Jesus' enemies did not deny them, they attributed them instead to the work of the devil. In performing miracles, Jesus confronted the various manifestations of evil in human life with a power that went far beyond the ordinary range of human experience. The certainty with which he acted and the conviction with which he spoke, signified on the part of Jesus a consciousness of a unique relationship with God. This superior power and authority was acknowledged by the people who encountered him (cf Mk 1:27-28). Furthermore, his relationship with God implied more than that of an agent: God was acting not only through him, but in him. The healing of all forms of evil made Jesus stand out from other healers, especially his giving of sight to the blind, which would have been seen as a characteristic of messianic times (cf Is 35:5-6).

The gospels also relate that Jesus had visionary experiences on the occasion of his baptism and transfiguration, as well as sayings that allude to similar experiences. Jesus evidently had some sort of spiritual experience at his baptism (cf Mk 1:9-11 and par). As God's anointed servant, Jesus was empowered by the Spirit to establish God's reign on earth. The transfiguration scene occurs as Jesus faced the prospect of death in Jerusalem (cf Mk 9:2-8 and par). These experiences cannot easily be dismissed as having no historical foundation.

Jesus was crucified as King of the Jews, as the title on the cross proclaimed. This title, however, does not reflect the way the early church addressed Jesus, evidently because of its political overtones. And yet the church would never have proclaimed Jesus as Messiah unless he had been crucified as a messianic figure. Something about the life and ministry of Jesus must have suggested to outsiders and opponents alike that Jesus was indeed a messianic figure who could prove to be politically dangerous.

This would explain why Jesus was put to death as King of the Jews. The disciples, like their fellow Jews, were not expecting a crucified and risen Messiah (cf Lk 24:21). Given this, their christ-ological reflections had to be reformulated and refined in the light of Jesus' crucifixion and resurrection, but they did not begin only at this point. They would already have begun early on in Jesus' ministry.

All this evidence, although admittedly indirect, does give the distinct impression that there was a messianic aspect to Jesus' life and ministry. Jesus would have been conscious of the fact and would have acted in a particular way because of it. He would have been careful at the same time of being cast as a revo-lutionary leader of the zealot type, or as a political claimant to the throne of David. There is, however, proof of a more direct nature in the gospels that Jesus used various titles in reference to himself and these reveal that he was the Messiah in a very spe-cial sense.

Son of Man. Most scholars believe that Jesus used the title Son of Man to refer to himself during his ministry. It appears over eighty times in the gospels in three types of settings: referring to his earthly activity, e.g., eating and drinking; to the suffering Son of Man; to his future glory in judgement. It is mostly found on the lips of Jesus. During the first century of the Christian era there was considerable speculation in Jewish circles concerning the Son of Man figure (cf 1 Enoch, IV Ezra), and Josephus' *Antiquities* informs us that the book of Daniel was popular at the time. The author of Daniel saw one 'like a son of man' (7:13), a representative figure, who comes into the presence of God. He is contrasted with the kings of the surrounding evil empires and so in some sense embodies Israel. He is also given a kingdom which makes him a royal figure. In the scene in Daniel he is being invested by God. In 1 Enoch and IV Ezra the 'son of man' is clearly an individual. That Jesus alluded to Daniel in his teach-ing would be natural given the association of the Son of Man with the kingdom or reign of God. The Daniel figure comes into God's presence at a time when his people are suffering at the

hands of evil empires. It is therefore not impossible that the prediction of a violent death of the Son of Man, which we find in the
gospels (cf Mk 8:31, 9:31, 10:33-34 and par), was announced by
Jesus himself, even if the actual gospel formulation is later. In
the scene before the High Priest in Mk 14:62, the reply of Jesus
has a clear reference to the book of Daniel when the Son of Man
is seated at the right hand of God (cf Ps 110:1), and will be seen
coming in the clouds of heaven. It seems then that Jesus' frequent use of the title implied a messianic self-understanding
that referred to both suffering and vindication. Given the fact
that Son of Man speculation was a live issue in the first century
among the Jews, Jesus' use of this title would have been comprehensible during his ministry.

Messiah. At the time of Jesus there was no normative concept
of what the Messiah should be, although a dominant conception
was of a royal or kingly figure. Accordingly, Jesus felt free to
give the term a new significance. When Peter acclaims Jesus as
Messiah (Mk 8:27-33), he enjoins his disciples to silence while he
goes on to speak of himself as the Son of Man who must suffer. It
was not that the designation Messiah was wrong, for Mark already had it in the title (1:1), but Mark's portrait wants to show
that before his suffering and death, Jesus did not want to accept
this identification without qualification lest his suffering be
overlooked. This hesitancy may well go back to the ministry of
Jesus. Disciples would have accepted him as Messiah because of
what he said and did. Jesus does not reject the title outright, but
qualifies it since he does not wish to be mistaken for a particular
kind of Messiah. When the High Priest asks him if he is the
Messiah, the Son of the Blessed One, Jesus affirms it, but redefines it by reference to the Son of Man (Mk 14:61-62; cf 15:2,26).
The frequency with which followers use the term 'Messiah' for
Jesus in the gospels makes it likely that it does go back to Jesus'
time, otherwise he would have been crucified on a totally false
charge. Yet he never accepted the attribution given it by disciples and opponents.

Son of God. Few scholars nowadays doubt that Jesus used

Abba to address God his Father (cf Mk 14:36). The term itself connotes intimacy even when used in relation to God. The gospels show Jesus is conscious of a unique relationship when he addresses God as Abba, Father. It seems that this way of addressing God was a characteristic of Jesus himself and he taught his disciples to do likewise (cf Lk 11:2). In the Old Testament 'son of God' designated a special relationship to the God of Israel on the part of the people, the king or virtuous individuals. The use of the term Abba by Jesus implied a degree of intimacy with God unprecedented in the Judaism of the time. Jesus saw himself as Son in intimate relationship with the God of Israel, and he was able to mediate a similar relationship for his disciples as well. It seems likely that Jesus spoke of himself as Son since this was crucial to his identity and status.

In Mt 11:25-27, Lk 10:21-22, Jesus thanks the Father for his unique revelation to him. Nobody knows the Father except the Son, and so Jesus is able to reveal the true identity of the Father to others. The parable of the vineyard (Mk 12:1-12) serves to confirm that Jesus regarded himself as the son and heir. In Mk 13:32 though, there is a strange saying that nobody, not even the Son, knows when the end of the world will come. The saying is in an apocalyptic setting emphasising that certain events are a divine secret. Yet it also indicates that Jesus saw himself as having more intimate knowledge than the angels and so he believed that he was Son in a very special sense.

Wisdom. Jesus presented himself to his contemporaries as a wisdom teacher using parables, proverbs and giving rules for living which were typical of the sages in Judaism. The queen of the south came to hear Solomon's wisdom, but in Jesus there is one greater than Solomon, the patron of wisdom (cf Mt 12:42). It is in his own name that Jesus promises the gift of wisdom to his followers (Lk 21:15). Misunderstood by his incredulous generation, Jesus says of himself: 'Yet wisdom is vindicated by her deeds' (Mt 11:19). In the wisdom literature of the Old Testament, personified Wisdom is entrusted with God's revelation to others (cf Prov 8:32-36). And Jesus combines sonship language with that of wisdom to convey to others how he viewed himself (cf Mt 11:25-27; Lk 10:21-22).

Early Church Christology

The form of Christianity that emerged among Jewish converts in Palestine in the decades after Easter is known to us indirectly through fragments of prayers, hymns and creeds that were used by Paul and other New Testament writers. In Rom 8:15 and Gal 4:6 Paul says that the Holy Spirit prompts the Christian to invoke God as Abba, following the example of Jesus himself, as the unique expression of Christian prayer. He is writing to mainly gentile Christians in the middle of the first century and so Paul forms a bridge between the earliest Christian communities and the gospels. All this suggests that already there was widespread use of the term Abba for God even among non-Palestinian, non-Jewish Christians. In 1 Cor 16:22 the Aramaic *maran atha* (Come, Lord!) indicates that at an earlier date Jewish Christians prayed to Christ as Lord. Closely allied with this is the confession 'Jesus is Lord' (1 Cor 12:3; Rom 10:9; Phil 2:11) which means that Jesus is the risen Lord *(Kyrios)*, the name bestowed by God on Jesus after the completion of his mission. In Rom 1:3-4 Paul says that Jesus became Son of God in power, having previously been Son of God in weakness. This evidence leads to the conclusion that early on in the church's life it was seen as appropriate to confess Jesus in the same way as God and call Jesus *Kyrios,* the title used in the Old Testament Greek translation for God. After his resurrection, Jesus assumed a lordship role when he was installed as Son of God in power by the Spirit. Jesus was expected to return as Lord and this was prayed for.

In the hymn fragments scattered throughout the New Testament Letters, we find evidence that christology developed out of early Christian experiences of the risen Lord in the context of prayer, community worship, as well as reflection on the Jesus tradition that was being handed down. Christological prayers, confessions and hymns used Old Testament source material, especially the psalms and wisdom hymns, together with Christian material on the life, death and exaltation of Jesus. These were composed by disciples, some of whom were undoubtedly close to Jesus during his ministry. Hymns celebrating Jesus' death and resurrection were composed from the Jesus material; those dealing with the Son's pre-existence and incarnation drew on the wisdom literature, while those having to do with Jesus' exaltation to God's right hand appropriated the royal psalms (cf Phil 2:6-11; Col 1:15-20; 1 Tim 3:16; Heb 1:2-4; Jn 1:1-14). In all of these hymns it is clear that the subject is a real human figure, Jesus of Nazareth, not some mythical figure. Christians who composed these hymns did so to praise the historical Jesus who had now become the divine Christ, while at the same time safeguarding belief in the one God. Jewish speculation on the relationship between personified Wisdom and God facilitated this christological development that took place long before the gospels or even the Pauline Letters came to be written.

Another possible source for christology is the 'Q' source material common to Matthew and Luke that consists principally of sayings of Jesus. It is assumed by scholars to have been compiled early on for pedagogical use. In it Jesus is depicted as a wisdom teacher and indeed as God's Wisdom incarnate.[4] It seems then that there were early Christian communities using 'sayings' collections such as 'Q' which were written by those steeped in the Jewish teaching tradition.

Jewish Christians also used the psalms and the prophetic literature to articulate a christology. This is evident in the earlier chapters of Acts. Although composed by Luke in the eighties, these chapters have an archaic air about them that go back to the early preaching. The sermons of Peter and Paul emphasise who Jesus was and is: he is Messiah, Lord and Son of God in the Father's presence in heaven, having been raised from the dead and exalted to God's right hand (cf Acts 2:32-33, 36; 5:31). The resurrection is described in terms of enthronement in heaven using the royal psalms that celebrated the coronation of the

4. Cf Ben Witherington III, *Jesus the Sage: The Pilgrimage of Wisdom,* Minneapolis: Fortress Presws, 1994, pp 211-36

Davidic king as God's adopted son. They did not, however, believe that at the resurrection Jesus received an identity he did not already have during his ministry. What they attempt to express is that through the resurrection, believers came to recognise aspects of Jesus that they either were not fully aware of, or had not fully appreciated, during his ministry. By the time the gospels came to be written in the last third of the first century, a more precise christology had become evident.

It seems then that the various gospel christologies are only attempts to draw out and describe something that was already present in the person and ministry of Jesus. He was such an impressive and powerful figure that the gospels were in no danger of saying too much about him. They were only groping towards an adequate articulation of who and what Jesus was. Accordingly, we can speak in terms of continuity between Jesus' self-presentation, the christologies of the early church and the portraits of Jesus we find in the gospels. Even when we approach the gospels critically, there is evidence that Jesus spoke of himself as Son of Man, Son of God, and God's Wisdom. There is indirect evidence that suggests some kind of messianic self-understanding. In the light of this, therefore, an impressive case is to be made for continuity between Jesus and his post-Easter followers in terms of how Jesus was to be evaluated. Early Jewish Christians were already worshipping not only God as Abba but Jesus as Lord and praying for his return. This was evidently an early post-Easter development.

Thus the origins of 'high' Christology, with its emphasis on the divinity of Jesus, go back to early Christian worship that incorporated the wisdom traditions and psalms into their hymns. Worship of Jesus and reflection on his life forced them to re-read the Old Testament in a new light and to appropriate texts for the purpose of expressing their faith in him. An example of this is the Prologue of John, which has developed further the ideas that were latent in the earlier christological hymns.

The Evangelists

How did the evangelists convey their more developed understanding of Jesus' person? Evaluations of Jesus were associated
with different moments of his life, e.g., conception, birth, ministry, death and resurrection. Looking at the New Testament, it
is possible to trace in a general way a development of christology beginning from the resurrection that moves back to his early
life and even to his pre-existence. The resurrection was seen as
God's decisive intervention that brought the disciples to full
faith in who Jesus was. In the light of that faith, they gradually
interpreted the earlier parts of his life. This development did not
create a christological meaning that never existed in Jesus' life,
they were merely articulating a reality already there. There was
already a growing understanding and appreciation of the identity of Jesus on the part of his followers, despite their slowness in
consciously recognising and articulating it.

Although the gospels present Jesus as Messiah, Son of Man,
Son of God and Lord during his public ministry, nevertheless, a
certain tension is evident between his life of lowly service and
his exalted status. In Mark 1:11 the declaration 'You are my
beloved Son, with you I am well pleased' is a combination of
Psalm 2:7 and the servant song of Isaiah 42:1, making Jesus both
Messiah/Son and lowly servant at the one and the same time.
Yet Mark goes on to describe a ministry in which no human
being acknowledges Jesus' Sonship, his identity is a secret
known only to the reader and to the demons (cf 1:1,24, 3:11, 5:7).
Even Peter's recognition in 8:27-33 shows his difficulty in accepting a Messiah that had to suffer. In the transfiguration scene
(9:2-8), the glory hidden throughout the ministry shines forth for
a brief moment. God speaks again, but the disciples do not comprehend. Mark is stating that only through his suffering and
cross does the full identity of Jesus become known. At the moment of death the centurion acknowledges Jesus as Son of God
(15:39).

In Matthew, Jesus' exalted status breaks forth on certain occasions and the disciples recognise who he is (e.g., 8:25). Since

Luke has a second volume, Acts, to vocalise a post-resurrection christology, his gospel portrayal of Jesus is similar to Mark's. In John though, the exalted Christ is so stressed that the humanity of Jesus is almost lost to view. The glory of Jesus is already manifested to the disciples at Cana (2:11). The Word became flesh and believers have seen his glory (1:14), yet a glory different from that with the Father (17:5). Already in chapter one the disciples confess him as Messiah, King of Israel, Son of God. Jesus claims unity and equality with God (10:30, 33) and the gospel ends with Thomas' confession (20:28). This exalted christology affects the way Jesus both acts and speaks during his ministry in John: e.g., he knows all things (6:70-71), he goes to his passion not as a victim, but in complete control to accomplish the Father's work.

These examples show that despite the fact that the four evangelists are in agreement that during his ministry Jesus was clearly Messiah and Son of God, the way they balance this with the misunderstood and rejected Servant varies considerably. Different pictures of Jesus emerge, e.g., Mark gives more insight into Jesus as true man, whereas John emphasises that he was divine. Matthew and Luke show that the identity of Jesus manifested in his public life goes back to the moment of his conception. Both relate Jesus' human identity as descendent of David to Joseph (Mt 1:20; Lk 1:27), his divine identity to his being conceived by Mary through the power of the Holy Spirit (Mt 1:20; Lk 1:35). In John, the Word who already existed with God before creation (1:1-2) and became flesh (1:14) is the Son (1:18). The absolute use of 'I am' throughout the gospel (e.g., 8:28, 58), used as the divine name in the Old Testament (e.g., Is 43:25), is on the lips of Jesus. This is not a Johannine invention, but an elaboration of what was already in the synoptics (cf Mt 14:27; Mk 6:50). More than any other gospel, John brings the divinity of Jesus to the fore, thus making more explicit what was implicit during Jesus' ministry. We have seen that Jesus gave the impression of one in a unique relationship with God which was not shared by other emissaries. It took time for the unfolding of that relationship to reach full expression and clarity.

What the gospel writers were doing was giving expression to and appreciating a reality that was already there in the life of Jesus and correcting any misconceptions about him. Gospel christology, though, is primarily functional to indicate the role Jesus played in bringing about God's salvation for human beings. Nevertheless, John's affirmation that the Word was God (1:1) already manifests a movement from the functional to the ontological, even though the earlier confessions were not devoid of ontological implications. This movement continued throughout the early centuries of the Christian era until the council of Nicea in 325 solemnly defined the divinity of Jesus. The council of Chalcedon in 451 solemnly defined his full humanity. Jesus is true God and true man. Nevertheless, there is the ever-present temptation to choose one of these over the other. Some people find it difficult to imagine that Jesus is divine and attribute the gospel portrait of him to popular legend. Others have difficulty accepting Jesus' full humanity and are embarrassed when the gospels relate that Jesus was thirsty or tired because he was divine. Since knowledge comes through nature and Jesus had two natures, divine and human, divine knowledge is not transferable to a human mind.[5] God and humans know in different ways. Jesus then did not have unlimited knowledge as a human being (cf Mk 5:30-32, 10:17-18, 13:32; Lk 2:40, 52). However, this in no way denies that he was divine; rather it acknowledges that he was truly human.

THE NATURE OF THE SOURCES

Early Christians were convinced that the crucified and risen one was none other than Jesus of Nazareth. Nevertheless, a certain tension exists in joining the historical appearance of Jesus with a presence that can be grasped and appreciated only from a faith perspective. We can ask if the proclaimed Christ in the gospels is the same as the proclaiming Jesus who preached in Galilee? Are the words attributed to Jesus in the gospels the actual words of

5. Thomas Aquinas, *Summa Theologiae*, III, q 9, a 1 ad 1

the historical Jesus? Since the story of Jesus in the gospels is told from the viewpoint of the resurrection, must we not distance ourselves from this viewpoint in order to get to the real historical Jesus?

There is today a willingness on the part of scholars to recognise a greater continuity between Jesus' lifetime and the gospel portraits of him than they were hitherto willing to concede. The age of scepticism finally seems to be coming to an end. Scholarly research is now free to make a positive contribution when it clarifies the historical circumstances of Jesus' appearance and activity, the basic features of his proclamation, and sheds light on the underlying claims of Jesus that opens the way to the Christ of faith. To enter this way, however, is only possible for those who are willing to believe in the resurrection of the crucified Jesus. For it is from this vantage point that the evangelists look back on the life and activity of the historical Jesus to illuminate his enduring significance for the believer.

The Gospel Genre

The word 'gospel' refers primarily, not to a book, but to the preaching of a message. In the Old Testament it was used to proclaim God's great acts on Israel's behalf. This good news of what God is doing is now proclaimed in and through Jesus for everybody. It involves the reign of God made present in Jesus' person and activity in forgiving sins, healing human infirmity, feeding the hungry, calming the storms and raising the dead, as well as in his teaching and parables. Yet Jesus did not produce any writing and the early Christian preaching that the reign of God was present in Jesus did not depend on writing, but on oral proclamation. So what are the gospels? They are the natural development from Christian preaching.

> On the whole we see that the 'gospel' is a very particular kind of genre that is hardly comparable to other literary products of its time. It came out of Jesus' activity, was born of Jesus' Spirit, and developed with a focus on Jesus, the earthly One who lives on with God and is present in his church.[6]

6. R. Schnackenburg, *Jesus in the Gospels: A Biblical Christology*, Westminster: John Knox, 1995, p 12

The clear theological emphasis and missionary goal of the gospels, their composition from community tradition and use in worship, set them apart from every other writing. What is narrated is meant to evoke a response of faith in the hearers (cf Jn 20:31). The raw material of the gospels ultimately reaches back to Jesus himself, despite later re-shaping and development of the material over the decades that spanned the period between Jesus and the evangelists.

The other three gospels depict a Jesus with different attributes and traits largely absent in the Markan portrait. In Matthew and Luke the public life of Jesus is preceded by childhood stories and is continued in the post-resurrection appearances. In John the picture of Jesus' earthly activity is included in a christological view that developed within the Johannine community. The slant is different depending on whether a particular gospel originated in a diaspora Jewish milieu or in the pagan world. Jesus Christ is present in all of the accounts, yet in each one he is presented differently. Since none of the evangelists attempt to separate the historical Jesus from the Christ of faith, our attention is drawn to the total picture of Jesus Christ presented by each evangelist in his own particular way.

So let us look at the Gospel of Mark, the one who took the initiative in the late sixties to put ink to parchment. What does his work reveal? He offers an account of the words and deeds of Jesus that took place in the late twenties or early thirties. However, the experiences of the early Christians in the intervening decades coloured his selection and presentation of the Jesus material, as did the problems besetting his audience. Expansion or explanation would be demanded because hearers no longer were Palestinian Jews but gentile converts for whom Jewish customs and ideas seemed strange. Matthew and Luke were probably written some fifteen to twenty years later and offer more of the Jesus tradition, especially the sayings of Jesus. They also betray experiences different from the Markan community background. Another expression of the Jesus tradition found its place in John at the turn of the first century, so different in presentation from the other three that scholars try to reconstruct the specific community history that lay behind the composition. In spite of their differences, each of the gospels seeks to preserve the memory of Jesus from being lost when eyewitnesses passed away.

It is as living Lord that Jesus finds embodiment in the gospels. They are distinguished from the rest of the New Testament by their explicit attention to the story of Jesus in the past though coloured by the faith convictions of the authors. The image of Jesus in each of the gospels is distinct, yet it is recognisably the same Jesus. Many Christians feel uncomfortable with such diverse portraits of Jesus. Unthinkingly, they equate truth with what is historical and insist on asking which of them corresponds to what actually happened. They assume that the gospels intend to report only facts and that truth is the correspondence between facts and their reporting. By this reckoning only one version can be true. But the truth about historical persons is much more complex and is best narrated by others. How much more in the case of Jesus who was crucified as a criminal, but, according to his followers, was raised from the dead to share God's own life and is now the living Lord of his church. Understanding such a mysterious person could hardly be simple or straightforward, since it has to do with personal identity revealed in the character of the person and in the manner of his existence, not just facts of time and place.

In the second century the church accepted the four gospels in all their diversity as witnesses to and interpretations of Jesus' person rather than as factually accurate biographies. The gospels speak the truth about Jesus' character because they are related by four reliable voices rather than one. They have often been likened to portraits. While photographs generally tell us less about character than physical appearance, portraits show us the 'truth' about the person inasmuch as they reveal something of the character or personality of the subject. In the case of Jesus we have four views that reveal different aspects of his person. The evangelists were constrained in their presentations by their communities' ongoing experience of the risen Jesus in their midst, and by the facts and memories of Jesus' life that circulated from the beginning in the church. As well as these, the significance of Jesus' life and death was being appreciated in the light of the Old Testament by the early Christians. The evangelists profited from the long period in which the memory of Jesus was handed down in the communities of believers. While there are certain discrepancies in chronological and geographical detail, the character of Jesus is confirmed both by the memory of the past and the continuing experience of him in the present, especially in community worship. The gospels then are neither simple reporting nor distortions of Jesus, but portraits of his character that result from long reflection and creative use of earlier traditions.

The Synoptic Problem

Even a casual reading of the first three gospels reveals such striking similarities between them that they have been called the synoptic gospels. As well as similarities there are also important differences. These similarities and differences have led to a discussion as to the interrelationship between them and this is known as the Synoptic Problem.[7] Most scholars today conclude that Mark was written first and that both Matthew and Luke used Mark independently in composing their own gospels. To this they added other memories of Jesus available to them. Some of this added material is so similar (e.g., Mt 18:12-14; Lk 15:4-7) that Matthew and Luke must have independently drawn on a common written source, mostly sayings and parables, which is now unavailable to us. This is known as the 'Q' source. Other kinds of material in Matthew and Luke are so different that they must have come from independent sources and are designated Special Matthew (e.g., Mt 1-2) and Special Luke (e.g., Lk 1-2) respectively. This explanation is known as the modified Two Source theory, and may be regarded as the best explanation for appreciating the similarities and differences among the synoptic

7. For a full discussion, see R. Brown, *An Introduction to the New Testament*, New York: Doubleday, 1998, pp 111-125

gospels although it does not solve all the difficulties.[8] John represents an independent stream of tradition from the time of Jesus that had little contact with the synoptics and was shaped differently. Our chief concern, though, is with the final form of the text that resulted from a complex oral and written process. For despite any literary interrelationships, each of the gospel narratives presents Jesus in a distinctive way and so must be appreciated on its own terms.

Stages of Gospel Formation
The gospels represent the crystallisation of memories from the early Christians going back to the time of Jesus. However, the memory of Jesus in the church was never simply a mechanical recall of information about him from the past, but a recollection of the past that shed light on the present as well. The one remembered from the past was also being experienced in the present and this in turn shed light on the memory of him from the past. The memory of Jesus was also affected by contact with the diverse and changing circumstances of the first generation Christians. The Christian movement grew by the establishment of communities across geographical and cultural boundaries. Since Christianity was from the beginning a missionary movement, there was an early transition from a predominantly Palestinian rural community to urban communities throughout the Roman Empire. Because the language of the empire was Greek, not Hebrew or Aramaic, there was the added problem of translation. The memory of Jesus was also affected to some extent by contact with other traditions, e.g., diaspora Judaism, Greek philosophy and religion. The growth of the church's self-understanding and its memory of Jesus were mutually shaping influences. Within the various communities themselves, preaching, worship, teaching as well as the threat of persecution and attacks by sceptical outsiders, affected the growth and stabilisation of the Jesus tradition. Among these, community worship was particularly important, especially baptism and eucharist,

8. For other solutions, see Brown, ibid

each of which attracted to itself a body of tradition. The eucharist included readings from the Old Testament, preaching and prayers in imitation of synagogal worship.

The memory of Jesus was also shaped by the experience of the communities as they endeavoured to live out the implications of their new identity as Christians immersed in a pagan world. Teachers sought to find precedents for community practices and guidance for community decisions. The selection and shaping of the memory of Jesus in the light of the Spirit was not seen as a betrayal or distortion. It was the result of a deeper insight and understanding of the past by those who continued to live in the presence of the risen Lord whose Spirit opened up a new appreciation of the past (cf Jn 14:25-26). Habits of memory also affected the handing on of traditions that were passed on in the form of short sayings and stories. Stereotyped patterns resulted from the process of retelling in oral form in community contexts. Very quickly the specifics of time and place were lost since what was important was the significant saying or deed of Jesus. Many of the stories in the gospels fall into these patterns, e.g., controversies, parables, aphorisms.

The most difficult memory of Jesus to appreciate and so requiring most interpretation was his death as a common criminal on the cross. All the gospels have passion narratives, by far the largest segment of the Jesus story. Scholars suppose that these narratives unfolded and were written down early on. Christians searched the scriptures, now seen in a new light (cf Lk 24:27), to enable them to place this experience of Jesus within their symbolic world in a way that made sense. Jesus' death was 'according to the scriptures,' Jesus was the suffering just one, vindicated by God.

Three stages, therefore, can be discerned in the formation of the gospels.[9] There is first of all the public ministry of Jesus during which he proclaimed the kingdom, worked miracles, inter-

---

9. 'An Instruction about the Historical Truth of the Gospels', *AAS* 56 (1964), DS 3999; Vatican II, *Dogmatic Constitution on Divine Revelation*, 5.19

acted with people, chose disciples to be with him who saw and heard what he did and said. Jesus accommodated his teaching to the mentality of his listeners to facilitate understanding and memorisation. It is their memories of Jesus' words and deeds, as well as his suffering and death, that supply the material for the gospels. The gospels as we have them, though, are not a record of this stage.

The second stage was the apostolic preaching about Jesus during the second third of the first century. Those who had seen and heard Jesus had their following of him confirmed through the post-resurrection appearances and coming of the Spirit. They came to full faith in the risen Christ and they vocalised this through various titles, e.g., Messiah, Lord, Son of God, Son of Man, Saviour. This faith in turn illumined their memories so that they proclaimed his words and deeds with enriched significance in the hope of bringing others to faith. Their preaching asserted the fundamental continuity between Jesus of Nazareth and Jesus Christ as Lord. The preacher of the kingdom now became the preached one. Very soon the group of preachers became enlarged beyond the original companions of Jesus and there was the challenge of adapting the preaching to new audiences and new environments. Community liturgy, catechesis and controversies with opponents also helped shape their memories of Jesus.

The third stage is the written gospels. It was from the stories and sayings that were shaped during the second stage that the gospels were written in the last third of the first century. By this time there would have been some other written material while the oral development of the Jesus story still continued. By the end of the second century the four gospels were attributed to apostles (Matthew and John) or companions of the apostles (Mark and Luke). Yet such attestation was more often concerned with the one responsible for the tradition preserved and enshrined in a particular gospel, i.e., the authority and so the reliability of the tradition, rather than the one who actually penned the text itself. The recognition that the evangelists may not have been eyewitnesses of Jesus' ministry explains many of the differences with regard to time and place among the gospels. Each evangelist arranged the material at hand in a logical and topical rather than chronological order to portray Jesus in a way that would meet the spiritual needs of the audience for whom he was writing. In their shaping and development of the Jesus material, the evangelists were real authors, not just compilers.

The gospels then are not literal or stenographic records of the ministry of Jesus. Decades of developing, shaping and adapting the Jesus tradition intervened. The error in any simplistic or fundamentalist approach to the gospels is to confuse the first with the third stage. In the intervening second stage what was remembered about Jesus from the first stage was subjected to a Christian reflection born of faith in Jesus as Christ and Lord. Indirectly the gospels supply evidence as to how Jesus was presented as Lord and Messiah in the second stage, and in that preaching how he was perceived to have been during his ministry in the first stage. The christology of Jesus' earthly ministry is implicit and indirect, but Jesus sowed the seeds during his ministry of what later came to be recognised about him.

The gospels were fitted into a simple sequence of the public ministry of Jesus: baptism, preaching in Galilee and beyond, journey to Jerusalem, passion and death. Each evangelist placed incidents from the life of Jesus where they logically seemed to fit, not always in chronological order. The choice of material and orientation of each gospel was determined by the theological outlook of the evangelist. The theological outlook of Matthew and Luke is much clearer because of the changes they made to the Markan material. As regards the Johannine theological outlook, the development of the pre-Johannine tradition seems to have lasted several decades and reached final form only at the end of the first century. Although it does preserve reminiscences of Jesus' public life, it has profoundly rethought and rewritten the Jesus traditions. All the gospels were written for particular audiences in Syria, Greece, Asia Minor and Rome. By the end of the second century, the church accepted all four and made no effort to harmonise their differences.

CONCLUSION

While on the human level we can describe the composition of the gospels in terms of the oral and literary processes that lay behind them, Christians nevertheless believe that the Spirit was also active in the whole process. We speak of the gospels as 'inspired', which is a specific way of recognising their unique, sacred character. Together with the rest of the New Testament, they were placed on the same level as the Jewish scriptures that now became the Old Testament.

An important moment in Christianity's self-understanding was its decision to accept certain writings and reject others. The process was a slow, natural one and not without controversy. The church accepted four gospels as multiple witnesses and interpretations of Jesus. By doing so it asserted that it recognised in them a unity that it could not discover in the writings it had rejected. It was not a matter of politics or ideology, as is sometimes asserted, but the very essence of Christianity based on the truth about Jesus that was at stake. The Jesus portrayed in the four gospels corresponded to the Jesus experienced in the lives of Christians. Together they accurately witness to the truth of Jesus, and have the capacity to mediate that truth to successive generations of Christians. We are confident that the community meeting in the name of the risen Christ through the centuries has not been mislead and we trust that the means Jesus chose to communicate with us are dependable and reliable.

CHAPTER TWO

The Gospel of Mark

INTRODUCTION

Mark is the shortest and probably the earliest of the four gospels. To him must be attributed the shaping of the Christian message into a narrative about Jesus. Mark knit together sayings and stories about Jesus into a single literary work beginning from his baptism in the Jordan and mission in Galilee, to his death and resurrection in Jerusalem. It is a simple story that grips the reader with its rapid pace. It is filled with conflict between Jesus and his opponents and ends with a passion account that dominates the gospel.

There is general agreement among scholars that Mark was written around the year seventy A D. Since the end of the second century the gospel has been attributed to Mark, the disciple of Peter and Paul, and identified with the John Mark of Acts. From the gospel itself, the author seems to have been a Greek speaker who was not an eyewitness of Jesus' ministry. He drew on the pre-shaped oral and probably some written traditions, and addressed it to a community that had recently experienced persecution and failure. His audience appears to have been Greek speakers who did not know Aramaic. They were non-Jews, since Mark has to explain Jewish customs, yet he could assume that they were familiar with the Christian tradition and had already heard a lot about Jesus. It is traditionally thought to have been addressed to Rome where Christians were persecuted by Nero. That the gospel originally ended at 16:8 is best attested in the oldest and most reliable manuscripts. Appearances of the risen Lord were appended by a later hand in 16:9-20 and these verses are considered to be canonical.[10]

10. Although the best manuscripts end at 16:8, others contain what is called the Freer logion, a shorter ending, or a series of appearance accounts

The best way to get acquainted with the Markan narrative is to read it through from beginning to end before concentrating on its christology. A brief outline followed by the storyline is given to enable the reader to appreciate its features and emphases that are highlighted in the text. Many scholars find a dividing point of the gospel in chapter eight. Having been misunderstood and rejected in spite of all he had said and done, Jesus, as Son of Man, begins to proclaim his suffering, death and resurrection as part of God's plan. Readers are to learn from Jesus' miracles and parables, but unless this is combined with his passion and resurrection, they cannot appreciate who Jesus really is or what it implies to be his followers. The outline to follow will enable readers to see the flow of Mark's thought.

OUTLINE

1. Jesus' Ministry of Preaching and Healing in Galilee (1:1-8:26).

(a) Preparation for the public ministry of Jesus by John the Baptist, an initial day in the ministry, controversy at Capernaum (1:1-3:6).

(b) Jesus chooses the Twelve, trains them to become his disciples by parables and miracles, is rejected in his hometown of Nazareth (3:7-6:6).

(c) Jesus sends the Twelve on mission, feeds 5000 people, walks on the water, controversy over Jewish traditions, healings in gentile territory, feeds 4000, is misunderstood by disciples, heals a blind man (6:7-8:26).

(16:9-20) known as the longer ending, which are a summary of the appearances found in the other gospels. Many scholars accept that Mark originally ended at 16:8, and that the other endings were later added by scribes. If so, Mark then did not record any appearances of the risen Christ, despite the fact that 14:28 and 16:7 set up an expectation of at least one appearance in Galilee. Mark's failure to do so would be a significant omission and it is noteworthy that more than one writer in the second century did not feel that 16:8 brought the gospel to an adequate closure.

2. The Mystery of the Suffering Son of Man, Death and Resurrection (8:27-16:8, 9-20).

(a) Peter's confession, three passion predictions, transfiguration, instruction of disciples (8:27-10:52).

(b) Jesus' Jerusalem ministry – entry, cleansing of Temple, teaching, eschatological discourse (11:1-13:37).

(c) Anointing of Jesus, betrayal by Judas, Last Supper, agony, trial, crucifixion, death, empty tomb (14:1-16:8).

(d) Resurrection appearances by a later hand (16:9-20).

STORYLINE

The opening verse serves as a title for the entire narrative: the good news of salvation in and through Jesus crucified and risen, who is now acclaimed by Christians as Messiah and Son of God. In the first half of his gospel, Mark prefaces the beginning of Jesus' public ministry with that of John the Baptist. There follows a ministry of preaching, performance of powerful deeds and teaching in Galilee. Although he attracts crowds, Jesus struggles with demons, misunderstandings and a hostile reception by official Judaism.

Already attested in the scriptures as God's messenger, John preaches in the desert a message to prepare the way of the Lord, namely Jesus, who is the mightier One. At his baptism the Spirit descends on Jesus enabling him to carry out his mission to liberate his people. A voice from heaven identifies him as God's beloved Son. He is tested by Satan and is victorious – a preview of his ministry. Jesus proclaims that the reign of God is being inaugurated in his ministry and so there is need for repentance as well as faith. 'Reign of God' is a symbol expressing Israel's hope for salvation when God would rule in justice and peace. After the call of four disciples, Mark describes the kinds of things Jesus did: preaching in the synagogue at Capernaum with authority, although the content is not stated; casting out demons; healings and prayer. The presence of evil visible in human affliction and suffering must be overcome. The demons paradoxically recognise who he is, but Jesus forbids them to make him known.

Even the cleansed leper is bound to secrecy because publicity would make it impossible for Jesus to circulate freely. Exorcisms present in dramatic fashion the ultimate purpose of Jesus' coming: to free humans from the tyranny of evil in all its manifestations.

At Capernaum Mark situates five controversies where opponents raise objections to Jesus' doings. The conflicts revolve around values in Jesus' ministry: his claiming to forgive sins and to heal, his association with sinners and outcasts, his compassionate interpretation of the Law to satisfy human need and healing on the sabbath. These lead to conflict with others who have different values and priorities. But a new age has dawned, it is time for new wine and new wineskins. Acting on his own authority, Jesus does not live up to the expectations of the religious leaders, and this gives rise to a plot by the Pharisees and the Herodians to get rid of him. Mark draws our attention to Jesus' passion at an early stage.

A summary shows that Jesus attracts people from far and wide and he cures their illnesses. He then summons twelve disciples to be with him as companions, so that he can send them out to preach and overcome evil, thus enabling them to participate in his work. Jesus' relatives do not understand his new lifestyle and want to take him home. Meanwhile scribes come from Jerusalem to accuse him of being in league with the devil. Jesus assures them that, on the contrary, the two kingdoms are locked in mortal combat, but Jesus will be victorious. It is an unforgivable blasphemy to attribute Jesus' working through the Spirit to the devil. His mother and relatives arrive, but with the proclamation of God's reign, Jesus' family is now extended to all who do the will of God.

There follows a collection of parables and sayings that illustrate the mysterious revelation of the reign of God. The parable of the seed and its explanation, the mustard seed, and the seed growing by itself, affirm that God's reign is often hidden and unnoticed, yet wonderfully triumphant despite obstacles and yields a bumper harvest. However, those not in sympathy with

Jesus cannot comprehend the deeper meaning of his words. Only the disciples are granted the revelation of the mystery of the kingdom because of their openness and faith. Jesus' purpose in telling parables is, according to Mark, an explanation of the negative results of his preaching. His quote from Isaiah reflects his awareness of the people's attitude. Certainly, Jesus' purpose in telling parables was not to confuse, as the sayings about the lamp and hidden things reveal.

Jesus and his disciples then cross the lake and encounter a turbulent storm before arriving in gentile territory to liberate a possessed man from a legion of devils. Just as sickness and affliction reflect the kingdom of evil, so also in the ancient worldview do the eruptions of nature. Jesus' calming of the storm, an action similar to God in the Old Testament, is seen as the act of one whom the winds and sea obey. The struggle of Jesus with the demoniac is dramatically told, but does not end there. Jesus proceeds to cure the man and sends him to proclaim what the Lord had done for him. Crossing the sea again, Jesus heals a woman with a flow of blood and raises the daughter of a synagogue official. Jesus returns the girl to ordinary life, but in the telling of it, Mark's readers are meant to see the father's request '... that she may be saved and live,' and the result that she 'rose,' as a foreshadowing of Jesus' gift of eternal life. Jesus subsequently returns to his hometown, Nazareth, but his teaching in their synagogue only produces scepticism. The townspeople remember him as a carpenter and know his family. His wisdom and mighty works make little impression on them.

After this the disciples are sent on a mission as an extension of Jesus' own ministry. The austere conditions make it clear that it is no human effort that effects results. During this, there is a flashback to the death of John the Baptist at the hands of Herod – a stark reminder of the cost of faithfulness, and a foreboding of the fate that awaits Jesus and the disciples who share in his ministry. With the return of the disciples from a successful missionary journey, one of his greatest signs informs us about the nature of Jesus' work. He miraculously feeds a massive crowd of hungry people. The story is told in such a way as to evoke many levels of meaning: it represents Jesus' divine power at the service of hungry people; recalls the manna in the desert; points forward to Jesus' actions at the Last Supper; and foreshadows the messianic banquet. In the following scene, the disciples labour fruitlessly against the turbulent waves until they are rescued by Jesus. The divine identity of Jesus is suggested against the Old Testament background of the Red Sea crossing and the divine name 'I am.' A summary of healings at Genesaret follows.

A controversy over ritual purity which Jesus' disciples do not observe affords Jesus an opportunity to set forth the intent of the divine law. Too narrow an interpretation becomes a human tradition and ends up frustrating the real intent of God's commandments. In the context of the reign of God, the Mosaic food laws are abrogated and Jesus declares that the moral defilement coming from within a person is the only cause of uncleanliness.

In sharp contrast to the hostility of the Jewish authorities is the faith of the pagan woman who, in spite of an apparent rebuff, refuses to be put off and is rewarded for her perseverance and sense of humour with the cure of her child. The healing of the deaf man and the feeding of the 4000 show that Jesus' extraordinary power is also at the service of pagans. Back in Palestine, the Pharisees demand a sign, not content with Jesus' miracles as heralding the advent of God's reign. As the Galilean ministry of Jesus comes to a close, the misunderstanding of the disciples only increases, ending in complete confusion about the significance of Jesus' words and deeds. The healing of the blind man at Bethsaida serves as a commentary on the situation: the man regains his sight in stages and this symbolises the gradual enlightenment of the disciples regarding the identity of Jesus.

In the second half of the Markan narrative, a change of pattern is detectable. Jesus now concentrates on instructing his disciples. He poses the key question by asking the disciples who do they think he is. The gospel of Mark has already been answering that question for the reader, yet Jesus' opponents have proven to be blind and the disciples to have been unable to grasp it. Peter

gives an initial acknowledgement by declaring him to be the
Messiah. But Jesus, while accepting this designation, prohibits
the disciples from making it known to avoid confusion with
contemporary ideas and expectations. His messiahship includes
the necessary component of suffering which Jesus now underlines with a prediction of his own fate. When Peter rejects this,
Jesus characterises his lack of understanding as a purely human
way of thinking and sets out the conditions for true discipleship.
There must be a willingness to take up the cross like Jesus did
and even a readiness to lose one's life for his sake. The
transfiguration scene gives bewildered disciples a glimpse of the
glory that Jesus possesses, though hitherto veiled, and a heavenly
voice identifies who he is. A subsequent discussion identifies
John the Baptist with the expected Elijah. The healing of the
epileptic boy, that the disciples were unable to effect, can only be
brought about, Jesus asserts, by prayer.

A journey through Galilee begins with the second prediction
of the passion, the significance of which the disciples fail to
grasp. This leads Jesus to instruct them on various topics by joining together key words or by association of ideas. The disciples
are not to seek the highest places, but are to be servants of all, especially the lowly, and this is exemplified by the reception of a
child in their midst. After an exhortation to broadmindedness, a
warning against scandal extends to the little ones, and the disciples are challenged to be like fire and salt – a purifying and sea-
soning presence. A question posed by a Pharisee is the occasion
for teaching on marriage and divorce. Jesus appeals to Genesis
for the unity created by marriage and forbids dissolution so that
remarriage constitutes adultery. The blessing of children brought
to Jesus creates an opportunity for instruction on the need for
receptivity. In response to the rich man's question, Jesus challenges him to sell his possessions, give the proceeds to the poor
and follow him, to which the rich man is unwilling to respond.
Jesus continues his instruction about those who make sacrifices
for his sake by assuring them that they will be rewarded.

After the third prediction of the passion, James and John vie

for the first places in the kingdom. But Jesus challenges them instead to share in his sufferings and adds that true greatness is
defined, not by lording it over others, but by giving one's life for
them. In all of this Jesus himself is the model who came, not to
be served, but to give his life as a ransom for others. The death of
Jesus is seen, not as a tragic failure, but as the ultimate expression of Jesus' entire mission, as an act of self-sacrificing love for
others. The journey towards Jerusalem has its final scene in
Jericho where Jesus heals blind Bartimeus who follows him
along the road to Jerusalem.

As Jesus enters the city, he is acclaimed as the king who will
restore the Davidic kingdom. The story of the cleansing of the
Temple is surrounded by the cursing and withering of the fig
tree. This is a prophetic sign signalling Jesus' judgement on
Israel's worship that is barren and so doomed. Jesus adds a lesson on faith, the power of prayer and forgiveness. When the
scribes and elders challenge Jesus' authority he tells them that
by their rejection of John the Baptist, Israel has incurred divine
judgement. This is confirmed by the parable of the vineyard tenants when the vineyard is given to the new Israel, the community
of disciples of which Jesus is the cornerstone. Jesus is questioned
about tribute to Caesar, resurrection, and the greatest commandment that stresses the love that is to be characteristic of disciples. Jesus poses his own question about Davidic sonship, and
ends by excoriating leaders who love the external trappings of
religion while guilty of extortion, and contrasts them with the
widow who gives everything.

Seated on the Mount of Olives, Jesus delivers his last discourse that looks to the future of his community and the end
time. It is a collection of prophetic warnings and apocalyptic
signs. The church must complete its mission of proclaiming the
gospel to the whole world. This will involve suffering and
persecution until the final moment of history when Jesus as the
Son of Man will return in triumph to gather his people and lead
them to God. In the meantime they are to be watchful.

Two long chapters show the importance of the passion for

Mark. Jesus' death for the sake of others sums up his entire mission and is the ultimate revelation of the Son of God. The passion narrative moves quickly to a climax. Jewish leaders, aided by Judas, plot his death while an unidentified woman anoints his body with a view to his burial. This is followed by preparations for the Passover feast during which Jesus, by breaking the bread and sharing the cup, offers living signs of his death for others, and Peter's denial is foretold. At Gethsemane Jesus prays for the strength to carry out God's will while the disciples sleep. Judas leads the band to arrest Jesus, while the other disciples flee in panic.

The trials before the Sanhedrin and Pilate dominate the narrative. Jesus is condemned by the Sanhedrin and mocked, while Peter denies him. When Jesus confesses that he is the Messiah and Son of God, the authorities accuse him of blasphemy and hand him over to Pilate to be crucified. Jesus is condemned, spat upon and mocked as King of the Jews by the soldiers. On the journey to Calvary, he is helped by Simon of Cyrene. Jesus is crucified while the passers-by, chief priests and criminals taunt him. He dies with Psalm 22 on his lips. The passion story provides the final answer to the question of who Jesus is. He is the Messiah, Son of God, Son of Man who liberates by giving his life for others. He is the Son revealed in the weakness of a human life totally committed to others. This is acknowledged by the pagan centurion at the moment of death when the veil of the Temple is torn in two. Jesus' body is buried in haste, but the women take note of where he is buried. Early Sunday morning, when they come to anoint the body, the tomb is already open and an angel announces that Jesus is risen. The disciples will see him in Galilee as he had told them. The women flee in fear and tell nobody. Here the gospel once ended, but an addition was inserted by a later copyist. It gives a general summary of the resurrection appearances found in the other gospels.

JESUS IN MARK'S GOSPEL

The Narrative as a Whole

Narrative Criticism[11] serves to throw light on the gospel of
Mark as story. His story concerns real people, is based on actual
happenings and Mark has brought all his storytelling techniques to bear upon it. He has succeeded in fashioning a story
with narrative, settings, plot, characters and rhetoric to per-
suade the reader to enter the world presented in the narrative.[12]
In Mark's story Jesus is the central figure who is filled with the
Spirit to inaugurate God's rule on earth. What Jesus does reveals
the extent and nature of his authority from God. What he says
discloses his understanding of himself as God's agent to accomplish his purposes. What others say about Jesus and how others
react to him reveal different aspects of his character as people
are amazed, take offence, remain loyal or fiercely oppose him. In
the story the portrayal of Jesus moves from one who is authoritative in word and deed to one who is rejected and eventually ex-
ecuted. But death is not the final word in Mark. Jesus is risen
from the dead, the tomb is empty.

The gospel of Mark displays its christology in two stages: the
period prior to Peter's confession that Jesus is the Messiah, and
the period following to the centurion's confession that he was
God's Son. In the first period, Mark focuses on Jesus as the powerful herald of God's in-breaking rule; in the second, on Jesus'
destiny as Son of Man who must suffer, die and rise from the
dead before returning at the end of the ages. As each stage unfolds, Mark builds up the character of Jesus so that by the end of
the narrative readers can appreciate the whole truth about the
reality of Jesus.

Before considering the titles for Jesus used by Mark, it is
worth examining his descriptions of the activity of Jesus who

11. Mark A. Powell, *What is Narrative Criticism?* Minneapolis: Fortress
Press, 1990.
Cf D. Rhode, J. Dewey, D. Michie, *Mark as Story: An Introduction to the
Narrative of a Gospel*, Second Edition. Minneapolis: Fortress Press, 1999.

appears in Galilee and later in Jerusalem.[13] Jesus is portrayed as
preacher of the reign of God and teacher; he is healer, exorcist
and miracle worker; he confronts and enters into conflict with
opponents; he undergoes suffering and death. All these stories
of Jesus' activity and interaction with various people contribute
in no small way to the painting of the Markan portrait of Jesus.

Preacher. The proclamation of the good news of the inaugur-
ation of the reign of God is clearly the most important task of
Jesus (1:14-15, 38-39). Closely linked with this proclamation is
the expelling of demons which is the outward, visible sign of the
in-breaking of God's reign. By battling against the kingdom of
demons, Jesus is advancing the kingdom of God. Far from being
in league with Satan, Jesus makes it clear that no kingdom can
stand for long if divided against itself (3:24). The healing of different afflictions and illnesses which were seen as part of the
kingdom of evil, advances the kingdom. In all of these the healing power of God is tangibly present and visible to all.

To help spread his message Jesus picks twelve disciples and
sends them out with his authority to preach and to heal. The result is that people repent and are healed (6:12-13). The impression made by Jesus' cures is so great that the news cannot be
silenced, even at his express command. It spreads beyond
Palestine, foreshadowing the expansion of the gospel to the
pagan world (cf 7:24-30). What is recounted in Mark by way of
example, will be fully realised in the worldwide preaching of the
gospel. Thus the Jesus who once proclaimed in word and deed
reaches beyond his historical particularity. Although Jesus generally limited himself to Israel, God's people, during his lifetime
and took precautions to keep his healings secret, the power of
his proclamation is so powerful that it is destined to reach the
ends of the earth.

Teacher. Mark also speaks of Jesus' teaching and he is addressed as rabbi, teacher, both by the disciples and by people at
large. Jesus teaches in the synagogue, in the Temple, by the
shores of the lake and in the villages of Galilee. He instructs

13. Cf R. Schnackenburg, *Jesus in the Gospels*, pp 17-73

large crowds because he felt compassion for them (6:34), and
people flock to him from beyond the confines of Palestine. Jesus'
teaching on a whole range of issues is still topical and relevant to
the life of the church. His teaching is not some abstract message,
but witnesses to a power that breaks into the earthly reality
where people live out their daily lives. This in turn demands appropriate behaviour and action on the part of those who accept
it. The reign of God inaugurated by Jesus becomes concretely
embodied in the life of his followers. Jesus' teaching from a boat
in the lake in the form of parables is a symbol of the community
of believers that must be instructed on matters that affect their
lives. Mark selected three growth parables as a sample of the
kinds of things Jesus taught that are still relevant for his hearers.
The parable of the scattered seed reminds the community of the
obstacles and dangers in accepting the word. Yet despite these,
it inspires confidence that God's word will prevail and bear
fruit. The allegorical explanation that follows concentrates on
the reception of the word by people with differing dispositions
who prepare bad or good soil for the word to take root. The sayings about the light and correct hearing are directed to the community who have accepted the message. The light received from
Jesus must be made manifest in word and deed.

The parable of the seed growing by itself places emphasis on
the power of God. It is like the earth bringing forth fruit in its
own time and manner. So too in God's own time the community
will grow and bear fruit. The parable of the mustard seed gives
an optimistic view of the reign of God when it will be fully established. As a dynamic entity it grows out of small beginnings
to encompass the whole world. This is a view of the mission of
the church in which the growth of the kingdom becomes transparent and tangible until it achieves its worldwide goal. What
Jesus teaches here is achieved in the church. In this way Mark
takes Jesus' proclamation of the reign of God and transfers it to
the time of the church. He goes beyond the historical framework
to reveal a picture that makes visible Jesus' ongoing presence in
the world.

)ugh Jesus is placed among the Jewish teachers of his time, he is, nevertheless, distinguished from them. Mark informs us that people are astounded at his teaching (1:22). After Jesus expels a demon, people exclaim: 'What is this? A new teaching! With authority he commands even the unclean spirits, and they obey him' (1:27). We are not informed about what Jesus taught, only how his teaching was received; it appeared as a new teaching with divine authority behind it, unlike the Jewish leaders. For Mark, Jesus continues to be the teacher of his community that he now instructs on matters of life and death. Only in this way can we appreciate why Jesus' suffering and death is also called a 'teaching' for the disciples (cf 8:31, 9:31). This teaching also included what believers are only able to comprehend in the light of Easter.

Healer. After Jesus' authoritative teaching in the synagogue at Capernaum on the sabbath, Mark has a summary report of his many healings and exorcisms (1:32-34). He gives examples of individuals healed by Jesus: Simon's mother-in-law, the leper, the paralytic, the man with the withered hand (cf 1:29-3:6). Later on in his narrative there is the healing of the demoniac, the woman with the haemorrhage, the raising of the daughter of Jairus (5:1-43). These are followed by another summary report (6:56). After this come cures of the daughter of the Syro-Phoenician woman, the deaf mute, the blind man, the epileptic boy and blind Bartimaeus (cf 7:24-37, 8:22-26, 9:14-29, 10:46-52). Thus the healings are distributed by Mark throughout the length of Jesus' public life right up to his entrance into Jerusalem.

These stories of healings offer an important ingredient for Mark's picture of Jesus. He is at one and the same time exorcist and healer from whom power exudes (cf 5:30, 6:56). The summaries suggest that exorcisms and healings were a typical feature of his work. They characterise Jesus as the bringer of salvation, as one who restores God's creation blessing, and ushers in messianic times. Mark sees them as signs associated with the time of salvation: 'And they were astonished beyond measure, saying, "He has done all things well; he even makes the deaf to hear and

the dumb to speak'"' (7:37, cf Is.35:5-6). God now eradicates afflictions and illnesses through Jesus, not only throughout the
land of Israel, but even in pagan territory. People are made
whole and ready for new life. Jesus is portrayed, not so much as
a miracle worker, but as one who mediates a power to cure that
comes from God. There is the command to silence lest God's
healing activity be publicised and misunderstood. Nevertheless,
the cures are so astounding that the news cannot be witheld.
People cannot but be aware of the impression these deeds make,
yet on the whole they, sadly, do not comprehend. They go so far
as to take offence at them (cf 6:2-3).

In the case of the woman who suffers from a flow of blood,
she touches his clothing secretly. Jesus feels power go out from
him and inquires who did it. When the woman confesses in fear
and trembling, he addresses her: 'Daughter, your faith has made
you well; go in peace and be healed of your disease' (5:34). Her
trust in Jesus' power has purified her faith in him and brought
her to experience God's peace. Faith and healing also go hand in
hand in the case of the epileptic boy who was possessed by a
spirit (9:14-29). To the distraught father's earnest plea, Jesus responds that all things are possible for one who believes. When
the father cries out: 'I believe; help my unbelief!' Jesus brings
about the cure of the boy. Jesus' healing power is now available
and effective in the church on condition that it perseveres in confident faith and prayer (cf 9:29).

Drawing on the traditions that were available, Mark sketches
a picture of Jesus as exorcist and healer which highlights the
healing power bestowed by God, but also shows Jesus' human
warmth and compassion for people in the grip of suffering. A
dominant characteristic is Jesus' closeness to the Father, to
whose power he appeals with confidence (cf.7:34). Jesus now
acts as Mark's proclaimed Messiah and Son of God. He is the
one who powerfully works to heal the wounds of human suffering as the above sample cases and the summaries amply demonstrate.

Miracle Worker. Mark has other extraordinary manifestations of power when Jesus calms the storm, feeds the hungry, walks on the water and is transfigured before the disciples. In the latter two episodes, the divinity of Jesus is barely concealed behind the figure of an authoritative earthly Jesus. He has already been proclaimed Son of God in the baptismal scene (1:11). But only in the transfiguration scene do the disciples hear the voice of God pointing to Jesus and saying: '... listen to him' (9:7). Within this earthly Jesus who proclaims the kingdom, teaches and casts out devils, is the future glory that will be revealed only at the resurrection. This explains Jesus' injunction to silence until the Son of Man is risen from the dead (9:9). Until that moment, the glory of Jesus, revealed briefly at the transfiguration, will not become apparent.

The stories of the calming of the storm (4:35-41) and walking on the water (6:45-52) may be described as epiphanies. In the Old Testament, it is God alone who rescues from the waters (Ps 144:7), and treads on the waves of the sea (Job 9:8). This superiority and power of God over the threatening waters of chaos is now transferred to Jesus. He rescues his disciples when he commands the wind so that a great calm ensues and when he climbs into the boat the wind dies down. In these two stories the divinity of Jesus begins to permeate the mask of the external event. Far from being a 'ghost,' Jesus is the one who possesses divine power, calms the turbulent waters and saves the disciples from distress.

In the two feeding narratives (6:34-44, 8:1-10) Jesus' compassion for hungry people is highlighted. The feedings themselves are described in such a way that makes them transparent for the later church when they gather together to celebrate the eucharistic meal. Jesus' deeds acquire a deeper significance that even the disciples do not grasp. They fail to understand the meaning of the miracles of the loaves (6:52, 8:17-21). In the multiplication of the loaves, the eucharistic celebrations of the church and the messianic banquet are already anticipated. The picture of Jesus that emerges from all this is of a compassionate saviour of people and caring Lord of his church.

Conflict with opponents. The ministry of Jesus is also marked by clashes and conflicts with the leaders of the people. At the beginning of the gospel there are five controversy stories (2:1-3:6) that demonstrate Jesus' superiority over his opponents. When Jesus assures the paralytic that his sins are forgiven, the scribes who are present secretly take offence, and think that Jesus is blaspheming. But Jesus proves through the healing of the paralytic that, as Son of Man, he has authority on earth to forgive sins. At the meal in Levi's house, the scribes attack the disciples because Jesus is eating with tax collectors and sinners, but again Jesus justifies his mission to sinners to whom he shows God's compassion and closeness. On the question of fasting, Jesus declares that the time of salvation ushered in by him is one of joy and celebration. The conflict over the plucking of grain involves a question of sabbath observance but is justified by Jesus: 'The sabbath was made for man, not man for the sabbath; so the Son of Man is lord even of the sabbath' (2:27-28). Conflict comes to a head with the sabbath healing of the man with the withered hand when the Pharisees join forces with the Herodians to eliminate Jesus.

The assault by Jesus' opponents intensifies with the Beelzebul controversy (3:22-30). Jesus' success in exorcising demons is attributed to Satan. But Jesus rejects this insinuation and warns that those who blaspheme in this manner are doing so against the Holy Spirit's power apparent in Jesus' healings. Jesus is misunderstood even by his own relatives (3:21) and the townspeople of Nazareth where he grew up (6:1-6) – that is, among the very people with whom he ought to have been able to find acceptance. His relatives do not understand his devotion and self-sacrifice for people; the townspeople are amazed at his wisdom and mighty works, but do not believe in him. The narrator adds that Jesus was astonished at their unbelief. Gradually the line of separation between believers and unbelievers is becoming clearer. It seems that the activity of Jesus for the benefit of others has the power to divide.

A new controversy about purity and ritual washing (7:1-13)

leads to a debate on the precepts and interpretations that had grown up around them. Jesus counters the scribes' attack on the disciples by noting that they nullify the commandments of God for the sake of their traditions. He gives an example of how the fourth commandment can be circumvented by casuistry. What defiles a person, Jesus says, is not what a person eats, but what comes out of the heart. There follows an instruction for the community about evil thoughts and actions. Jesus is here portrayed as the moral teacher in confrontation with the Jewish understanding of the Law. Later on the Pharisees demand from Jesus an extraordinary confirmation of his mission by some heavenly sign which Jesus refuses (8:11-13), and he goes on to warn the disciples about the evil mindset of the Pharisees and Herodians. The disciples, however, fail to understand Jesus' allusion, and are in danger of losing faith because of their earthbound mentality and lack of attention to the significance of Jesus' deeds.

The conflict with opponents becomes acute as Jesus journeys towards Jerusalem and sees suffering and death looming in front of him. Three times he announces the fate that awaits him (8:31, 9:31, 10:33-34). Mark symbolises the conflict with Judaism in the cursing and withering of the fig tree. In between is placed the cleansing of the Temple (11:12-21), and so the cursing becomes a prophetic protest against cultic rituals carried out in the Temple. Israel, the fig tree planted by God, is unfruitful and is condemned. In contrast to an unbelieving and unfruitful Israel, the Christian community is to place its trust in God through faith, perseverance in prayer and forgiveness. The quotation from Isaiah 56:7 points to a community made up of all peoples. The chief priests and scribes react by seeking a way to get rid of Jesus (11:18), and demand to know by what authority he is acting. When Jesus poses a counter-question about John's baptism, they are reduced to silence.

The parable of the wicked tenants (12:1-12) is a thinly-veiled attack on the Jewish leadership which routinely persecutes and kills God's emissaries. The parable reaches a climax in the sending of the son and his murder by the tenants. For Mark's

Christians the meaning is clear: it was the enmity of the Jewish leadership that brought about Jesus' death. Now God will take the vineyard from them and give it to others, i.e. to the Christian community. Jesus is the beloved Son of the parable who, after his death, becomes the cornerstone of the new house of God. What follows shows the continuing tension between Jesus and the leaders of the Jews (12:13-37) as they try to trap him in his speech. The issues under discussion serve also as instruction for the Christian community: poll tax, resurrection, the greatest commandment, the sonship of David. Jesus shows his superiority in arguing with opponents as well as giving guidance for his church, especially in the love commandment that is to charac-terise his followers. Jesus is more than the son of David, he is Lord whom God himself addresses through his Spirit in the scriptures (12:36).

Suffering and Death. Confrontations and conflicts permeate the whole narrative of Mark until it reaches a climax in the pro-ceedings before the Sanhedrin. The High Priest's solemn interrog-ation: 'Are you the Messiah, the Son of the Blessed One?' (14:61) is answered by Jesus with a clear 'I am' and he adds: 'You will see the Son of man seated at the right hand of the Power, and coming with the clouds of heaven' (14:62). Jesus now openly confesses his messiahship with the added reference to the Son of Man. There is a clear allusion to Psalm 110:1 and Daniel 7:13, two important reference points for New Testament christology. The High Priest clearly understood the implications when he accused Jesus of blasphemy.

For Mark, Jesus is Messiah, Son of God and Son of Man who, according to Daniel 7:13-14, will come one day in power and glory as Lord and judge. This revelation occurs at the very mom-ent when Jesus' fate is being decided. Jesus is the one living with God to whom the Christian community looks, and whom they expect to come again as the Son of Man. Mark's presentation reaches its culmination in the passion which forms a lengthy part of his narrative. He guides us through the trial to the climax of his death with Jesus' anguished cry as he breathes his last, to the rending of the Temple veil and the confession of the centurion. Mark appropriates material that came from the early church. Several aspects of his passion account stand out.

There is first of all his lengthy presentation of the nocturnal hearing against Jesus, the trial before Pilate and the carrying out of the death sentence. This is preceded by the betrayal of Judas, the visit to Gethsemane and the arrest there. There is also the picture of Jesus illumined by interpretation. In the three passion predictions Jesus was the Son of Man who must suffer, be rejected and betrayed. This now reaches a deeper dimension with the Son of Man addition inserted into the passion story (14:62). A contrast between the failure of the disciples and the denial of Peter on the one hand, and the Son of Man who consciously embraces suffering and death as the suffering righteous one, is evident. Suffering and death are viewed by Mark as a passage to resurrection. Already as they descended from the mountain of the transfiguration, the disciples were warned to tell no one until the Son of Man is risen from the dead (9:9). The resurrection is also included in the three passion predictions and reaches its climax in the message of the angel to the women at the tomb (16:6). Finally, there is the close connection between Jesus' suffering and discipleship, something that has already been made clear by the necessity of giving one's life for the sake of the gospel (8:34-37). The Christian is obliged to follow the path of service and suffering (10:35-45). The linking of the church with the suffering Jesus is also clear from the Last Supper as a meal that preserves the memory of his suffering and death when Christians partake of the body of Jesus and the blood of the covenant. The admonition to the disciples to watch and pray lest they enter into temptation (14:38), is told with an eye to the church which, like Jesus, must also go through trials and suffering. For Mark the death of Jesus is also the birth of the new community of salvation. This is signalled by the tearing of the veil of the Temple which points to the abrogation of the old cult (cf.11:17).

The picture of the persecuted, suffering and dying Jesus fills

out the portrait of Jesus whom the church confesses as its crucified and risen Lord. For Mark, though, the risen one remains the
crucified one: 'You are looking for Jesus of Nazareth, who was
crucified. He has been raised, he is not here. Look, there is the
place they laid him' (16:6). The portrayal of Jesus as preacher,
teacher, healer, exorcist, miracle-worker, as one who confronts
opponents, reaches its culmination in the passion and cross.

Titles of Jesus

Son of God. Jesus is called Son of God or its equivalent altogether
some ten times throughout Mark's gospel. It is likely that Mark
appropriated this title from the early Christian tradition, but
what does Mark wish us, the readers, to understand from his
use of it? It is mentioned at important points throughout the narrative. At the moment of death, the pagan centurion confesses
Jesus as Son of God. In fact, the gospel is framed by the confession of Jesus as the Son of God (1:1, 15:39). It is as Son of God that
he carries out his mission of inaugurating the reign of God
which reaches a climax in his passion and death.

Early in the gospel at the baptismal scene, the heavenly voice
reveals Jesus' status and dignity: 'You are my beloved Son, with
you I am well pleased' (1:11). Various Old Testament texts (cf Ps
2:7; Is 42:1; Gen 22:2) are amalgamated to form a uniquely new
picture of the beloved Son whom God has chosen. The heavens
are split open and the Spirit descends on Jesus in the form of a
dove. In the Old Testament the opening of the heavens so that
God could descend was seen as an eschatological event (Is
63:19). This is now fulfilled through the Spirit descending on
Jesus. The Spirit in turn designates the anointed one, the
Messiah (cf Is 11:2, 61:1). The difference now, however, is that
the Messiah is no longer the servant of God, but his beloved Son
who stands in close relationship with God. Jesus is the Messiah
to be sure, but much more (cf 12:35-37), for he far exceeds Jewish
hopes and expectations. This picture of the beloved Son of God
is of one who will cast out demons and engage opponents. The
designation is placed before Mark's readers right at the beginning

of Jesus' public appearance. It serves the purpose of giving an orientation for understanding Jesus' healings and exorcisms and his proclamation of God's reign.

The devils acknowledge his divine status and power, but Jesus emphatically forbids them to make him known. He does not want his identity revealed by spirits hostile to God and to the establishment of his reign. The Son of God also enters the mystery of suffering and death as God's lowly servant. It is precisely at the moment of death that the pagan centurion makes his confession. The Spirit-filled Son of God moves towards his death, but is raised up by God. That is why we, the readers, are invited to listen to him (9:7). In the eschatological discourse, the 'Son' is distinguished from the Father who alone knows the eschatological hour (13:32). This is in an apocalyptic context dealing with the imminent expectation of the parousia, yet it also speaks of not knowing the time when the end will come. The Markan text is emphasising that knowledge of the time of the parousia is a divine secret reserved to God alone. It is interesting to note that there seems to be a tension between the Son of God christology and this saying concerning the Son: 'But about that day or that hour no one knows, neither the angels in heaven, nor the Son, but only the Father' (13:32). The reason is because for Mark, the Son of God in his human nature must remain obedient and lovingly subordinate to God his Father.

The High Priest forges a link between Messiah and Son of the Blessed One (14:61-62), for the Jews could also call the Messiah the (adopted) son of God (cf Ps 2:7). Understood now in a Christian sense, they both point to the unique relationship of Jesus to God. Jesus answers affirmatively, but corrects the Jewish notion of Messiah by adding that he is also the Son of Man sitting at the right hand of God and coming in the clouds of heaven (14:62). Jesus, the Son of God, is to be exalted to God's side and will come again in power. The title Son of God for Mark summarises who Jesus is at work here on earth. He is the one equipped by God with the Spirit and with power, yet as servant goes obediently to the cross. In his activity the secret of the Son of God who is close to the Father is made visible, though it is still veiled and incomprehensible to those who witnessed it. The title Son of God is at the heart of Mark's estimation of who Jesus is.

Son of Man. The title Son of Man occurs some fourteen times in various contexts throughout the gospel. It refers to Jesus' earthly activity, his suffering and death, and his future functions. It is found mostly on the lips of Jesus himself. What is the self-understanding of Jesus concealed behind this designation? Mark connects the title with the person of Jesus and relates it exclusively to him. What special traits become visible in the Markan use of the Son of Man, and what do they add to his portrait of Jesus? What is the relationship between the Son of God and the Son of Man?

In eight places, the Son of Man sayings occur in a context of suffering and dying which Jesus is to undergo because of a divine necessity based upon the scriptures. The death of the Son of Man is necessary as a prelude to his rising from the dead that is included in all three passion predictions (8:31, 9:31, 10:33-34). In accordance with the will of God, Jesus must die but will rise again from the dead. The Son of Man undertakes this path of suffering as the innocent, persecuted, righteous one: 'For the Son of Man goes as it is written of him, but woe to the man by whom the Son of Man is betrayed! … The hour has come, the Son of Man is betrayed into the hands of sinners' (14:21, 41).

There is an aura of majesty also associated with the Son of Man sayings. After a period of great suffering followed by cosmic signs, the Son of Man will come in the clouds of heaven to gather his elect from the ends of the earth (cf 13:26-27). Here the vision of the one like 'a son of man' mentioned in Daniel 7:13 is applied to Jesus. In Daniel it is given a representative interpretation (cf 7:27), although it is evidently an individual of regal status, since he is being given a kingdom. In later apocalyptic writings (1 Enoch 46; IV Ezra 13) it is clearly an individual that is envisaged. This text became important in the early church to substantiate Jesus' claim as future judge: 'You will see the Son of Man seated at the right hand of the Power and coming with the clouds of heaven' (Mk 14:62). For Mark, therefore, Jesus is the Son of Man expected in the apocalyptic writings who will come as judge and saviour to gather his elect. At his parousia, Jesus will appear in power and glory, a power already possessed by the risen Jesus, which will now become cosmically visible and will be seen by all people. By applying the title Son of Man, Mark offers a perspective on Jesus that allows his journey towards death to end in glorification at the resurrection, and opens up a vision of the eschatological coming of Jesus as judge and saviour at the end of time.

Other passages in Mark portray the Son of Man active on earth. To the paralytic he grants forgiveness of sins before restoring him to health, 'that you may know that the Son of Man has authority on earth to forgive sins' (2:10). In doing this, Jesus is claiming an authority that belongs to God alone. Jesus' majesty is even now breaking through in his earthly ministry. It is one and the same Jesus already at work on earth who will also come in the future. The Son of Man is Lord also of the sabbath (2:28). As divine emissary he is above the Jewish interpretations of the sabbath commandment. He has divine authority not only to forgive sins and interpret the sabbath commandment, but also to regulate moral behaviour (cf 7:14-23).

As well as the foregoing assertions, paradoxically, the Son of Man is also the servant who gives himself for the sake of others: 'For the Son of Man also came not to be served but to serve, and to give his life a ransom for many' (10:45). Jesus in his humility becomes a model for renunciation of power and self-assertiveness (cf 10:42-44) which reaches a climax in his self-sacrifice on behalf of others: 'This is the blood of the covenant which is poured out for many' (14:24). Thus the humility and atoning death of Jesus is included in the Markan Son of Man christology. As Son of Man, Jesus can be seen in his earthly activity, at the same time, majestic and humble. All three dimensions of the Son of Man concept – his future coming in power and glory, his journey through suffering and death to resurrection, as well as his present work on earth – find expression in Mark's christology, but his emphasis is clearly on Jesus' suffering, death and resurrection.

Messiah. Other designations of Jesus used by Mark include Messiah, King of Israel, King of the Jews, Son of David, all of which are more or less equivalent. The most important of these is Peter's confession that Jesus is the Messiah (8:29). Yet Jesus forbids the disciples to speak about it. The reason for this apparently is to avoid a false understanding since 'messiah' could be conceived in purely earthly, political terms. In the Son of David discussion (12:35-37), Jewish expectations are transcended, and in the eschatological discourse Jesus warns against false messiahs who will lead the people astray (cf 13:21-22). The High Priest asks if Jesus is the Messiah, apparently with evil intent (14:61), while the chief priests and the scribes taunt Jesus to come down from the cross if he really is the Messiah (15:31-32). According to Jewish expectations, the Messiah would be a descendent of David, the king of Israel who would defeat Israel's enemies and restore the kingdom of Israel. Clearly Jesus did not fit this description. In the trial before Pilate he is accused of being king of the Jews to which he evasively answers: 'You have said so' (15:2), since it is directed towards a political claim. As king of the Jews he is mocked by the soldiers (15:17-20), and is crucified with an inscription over his head declaring the charge against him (15:26). This misinterpretation of Jesus as a political messiah, therefore, makes the title less suitable for Jesus according to Mark, for whom the crucified one is not a political rebel, but the Son of God.

Accordingly, the gospel of Mark redefines messiahship in terms of suffering, death and resurrection. It replaces the royal Davidic descendent who would defeat Israel's political enemies with a Messiah who must fulfil his destiny as Son of Man. Prior to his death and resurrection, even the disciples are unable to comprehend this mysterious Son of Man. Jesus is Messiah because he is Son of God who must suffer, die, rise from the dead and return as Son of Man, not because he is David's royal descendent. The Messiah is God's Son rather than David's. In

14:61-62, Mark's major christological terms – Messiah, Son of God, Son of Man – converge for the first time. Mark's narrative then defines messiahship in the light of Jesus' ministry, death and resurrection. It is defined in terms of Jesus, not vice versa. Although Jesus does not fulfil traditional expectations, his life and ministry are the norm for defining what it means to be God's anointed one.

The title Son of David in contemporary Jewish understanding was an equally unsuitable one for Jesus according to Mark. At the entry into Jerusalem, the people express their hopes for the coming kingdom 'of our father David' (11:10), but this expectation is left open. The superiority of Jesus over David is reflected in the scene of plucking grain on the sabbath (2:23-28). If David did something which was forbidden by the Law, how much more the Son of Man who is Lord of the sabbath. The insistent shouts of blind Bartimeus: 'Son of David, have mercy on me!' (10:47-48) are an expression of popular belief which Mark allows to stand, for it does not necessarily mean that Jesus accepts this title in its narrow connotation. It appears then that the title Son of David does not play an important role in Mark's portrait of Jesus. Like the other equivalents, it plays at most a secondary role.

Other Titles. The title Lord is important for Mark. In 12:36-37 Jesus is declared David's Lord and this designation is now obvious in virtue of his being raised from the dead to the side of God. During his ministry, Jesus is often addressed as Lord by others. This at least shows their esteem for Jesus, but Mark's readers would understand it in a deeper sense. The cured demoniac is told by Jesus to return to his people and tell them how much the Lord in his mercy has done for him, but he goes off and proclaims what Jesus had done for him (cf 5:19-20). However, Jesus as Lord does not become fully transparent until his exaltation to God's right hand.

John the Baptist announces Jesus as the 'more powerful one' (1:7) and in 3:27 Jesus is designated as the 'stronger one' who overcomes Satan. Jesus expels demons through the power of the

Spirit (cf 3:29). When he returns to his hometown of Nazareth, Jesus compares his reception there to that of a prophet (6:4). But if Jesus is popularly regarded as one of the prophets (cf. 8:28), it does not fully correspond to the claims he makes. He is more than a prophet and accepts Peter's designation of him as Messiah albeit with reservations. It seems then that all the minor designations of Jesus that we find in the narrative are inadequate to express Jesus' true status according to Mark. Only Son of God, Son of Man, and Messiah properly understood, do full justice to Jesus' self-understanding. For Mark they reflect the claims that Jesus made during his earthly ministry at least implicitly if not incohatively explicit.

The Messianic Secret

The messianic secret is so called from the several instances where Jesus commands people to be silent about his action or identity. The whole thrust of Mark's gospel makes it clear that the true meaning of Jesus' messiahship reaches clarity only with his death and resurrection. Throughout the narrative people who have been cured by Jesus are commanded to keep silent, though this is often ignored. Many scholars today would accept that Mark already found this in the tradition available to him. The demons must not reveal who he is or proclaim him as Son of God. In some of the healing stories the command to silence is absent. This would be pointless when large numbers witnessed the cure. Although Jesus wanted to preserve his secret, it was almost impossible to prevent an unusual healing from becoming public knowledge. Nevertheless, the injunction to silence, even though often disregarded, becomes a part of Mark's christology.

Mark shows that there was indeed a necessary and intentional veiling of Jesus' true identity until after Easter. In this it seems that he has retained a key historical element from the ministry of Jesus, i.e. that Jesus' self-disclosure came in an indirect manner involving both hiddenness and revelation to certain people (e.g. Mk 9:2-8). Occasionally, the veil is partially pulled back during the ministry, but there were no fully-fledged Christians before the death of Christ.

Accordingly, Jesus commands demons to be silent even though they recognise who he truly is, and they obey. Jesus evidently does not wish his identity to be proclaimed by demons who are opposed to the establishment of God's reign. This gives rise to a certain tension between his acts of power performed during his ministry, and the concealment of his identity in the earthly picture of Jesus. He prohibits even his disciples from publicly confessing him after Peter's identification (8:30) and after the transfiguration (9:9). Peter's confession of Jesus as the Messiah could be misconstrued to render Jesus a political liberator as the two sons of Zebedee evidently imagined him to be (cf 10:37). Although Peter's confession does represent a high point in the gospel, it is not totally acceptable to Jesus, and he forbids him from publishing it abroad. In the second half of the gospel, Jesus reveals to his disciples through word and deed that his messiahship entails suffering and death. Only when the Son of Man is risen from the dead is the secret to be revealed (9:9). It is from the vantage point of the resurrection alone that Jesus' messiahship and true identity can be properly appreciated. The secret, therefore, has a time limited purpose.

Another prominent feature associated with the secrecy motif is the disciples' extraordinary lack of understanding even in the face of the miraculous (cf 2:12, 5:42). Jesus' walking on the water does not lead to faith, only to unbelieving obstinacy (6:52). We would have expected that the first feeding miracle would have led to a recognition of who Jesus is, but the disciples are unable to understand because their hearts are hardened. In 8:14-21, the disciples' failure to understand is highlighted as ultimately a lack of faith that grows out of a failure to appreciate the revelation that is occurring through Jesus. The miracles of the loaves ought to have opened their eyes, but the disciples seem to have a zero comprehension of their significance. This is emphasised by the series of challenging questions posed by an exasperated Jesus. The motif seems to have been already present in the tradition, but amplified by Mark to teach his community a lesson.

Mark especially underlines the disciples' failure to understand Jesus' suffering and death (8:32; 9:32). This was important for a church called to discipleship of the crucified Jesus. Only in the light of the resurrection does the path to suffering and death make any sense (9:9-13). There is special instruction for disciples (cf 8:34ff) which also has relevance for the later church. During his earthly life, Jesus manifested himself through words and deeds. In the post-Easter period, he becomes recognisable for the church only if it accepts the earthly way of the Son of Man, and understands it as a call to shape its own life in conformity with that of Jesus (cf 8:34-38).

In the teaching on parables, the disciples are given an understanding while the deeper meaning is hidden from outsiders (4:11-12). It is the disciples who, in the post-Easter period, will have to accept responsibility for instruction in the church. Outsiders do not understand because of their lack of faith as the quotation from Isaiah makes clear. During his ministry Jesus spoke in parables, the surface meaning of which was easily comprehensible. But for a better appreciation of their full meaning, this symbolic language had to be explained by Jesus (4:33-34).

In Mark's gospel, then, various perspectives are presented. There is the lack of appreciation of who Jesus is in the pre-Easter period, and the danger of not wanting to understand the role of suffering and death. The gospel gives the community a basis for an appreciation of the person of Jesus that becomes possible only in hindsight. Mark's picture of the earthly Jesus gains in clarity for people of faith, but only after the resurrection. Mark paints a many-sided, not always harmonious portrait of Jesus drawing on the traditions available and moulding them to highlight his own accents. His christology can be summarised in terms of Messiah, Son of God, Son of Man, and yet none of these can be properly understood apart from his narrative. For the christology is in the story, and it is through the story that we learn to interpret the titles.

CHAPTER THREE

The Gospel of Matthew

INTRODUCTION

The position of Matthew in the ancient codices as the first of the gospels shows the esteem in which it was held by the church. This is accounted for by the addition of the infancy narratives and resurrection appearances as well as five long discourses of 'sayings' material mostly absent in Mark. Otherwise, Matthew produces up to ninety per cent of Mark, and much of the story-line is parallel to it. Yet it is worthwhile going through the text of Matthew to appreciate the flow of his story which is facilitated by his organisational skill and clarity of presentation. If we accept the priority of Mark, then he is Matthew's principal source into which he incorporated a collection of Jesus' teaching (Q), as well as his own special material (Special Matthew). Matthew gives strong emphasis to Jesus as teacher as well as relating him to the Old Testament by means of fulfilment quotations. In this way Jesus' whole life lay within God's preordained plan already revealed in the scriptures. Matthew, then, drew on existing materials to produce an original narrative and a distinctive portrait of Jesus.

Written some fifteen years or so after Mark, the gospel acquired prestige early on because of its association with the apostle Matthew. However, since the author of the final text seems to have used most of Mark, it is improbable that in its present form the gospel is the work of an eyewitness apostle. As related by Eusebius, Papias (c 130 AD) suggested that Matthew was associated with the gospel tradition: 'Matthew compiled the sayings in the Hebrew language, and everyone translated them as best he could.' If we accept the truth of this statement, it still leaves unresolved who wrote the full gospel in Greek, which is not a translation from either Hebrew or Aramaic. If the Greek Matthew is the original gospel, it is difficult to see how, in its present form, it can be attributed to Matthew, one of the Twelve. From the gospel itself, the author was evidently a Greek-speaking Jewish Christian who knew Aramaic and Hebrew, and was familiar with the Old Testament. Yet he was hardly an eyewitness to Jesus' ministry since he drew extensively on Mark and the 'sayings' source (Q), as well as other traditions. Scholars associate the gospel with Antioch in Syria, which had a large Christian community and was an important city of the Roman empire. The impression given is that the author was addressing a Jewish-Christian church that was rapidly becoming more gentile, a church that had all but severed ties with Judaism.

OUTLINE

The infancy narrative serves as a preface to Matthew's account of Jesus' ministry that reaches a climax in the paschal events. In between are five lengthy discourses alternating with narrative sections.

Introduction: The Origin and Infancy of Jesus (1:1-2:23)

(a) The who and how of Jesus' identity: genealogy and conception (1:1-25)

(b) The birth and destiny of Jesus: magi, flight into Egypt, massacre, return to Galilee (2:1-23)

I Preaching of the Kingdom in Deed and Word (3:1-7:29)

(a) Narrative: John the Baptist's preaching, baptism of Jesus, temptations, beginning of Galilean ministry (3:1-4:25)

(b) Discourse: Sermon on the Mount; beatitudes, teaching about the Law, almsgiving, prayer, fasting, judging others, true discipleship (5:1-7:29)

II Ministry and Mission in Galilee (8:1-10:42)

(a) Narrative: miracle stories intermingled with discipleship stories (8:1-9:38)

(b) Discourse: mission sermon; sending out of the Twelve, persecutions, conditions of discipleship (10:1-42)

III Opposition to Jesus and Teaching on the Kingdom (11:1-13:52)

(a) Narrative: Jesus and John the Baptist, reproaches on unrepentant towns, sabbath controversy, Jesus' family (11:1-12:50)

(b) Discourse: parables of the kingdom (13:1-52)

IV Jesus, the Kingdom and the Church (13:53-18:35)

(a) Narrative: rejection at Nazareth, death of John the Baptist, feeding of 5000 and walking on the water, controversy with Pharisees, healings, feeding of 4000, Peter's confession, first passion prediction, transfiguration, healing of a boy with demon, second passion prediction (13:53-17:27)

(b) Discourse: sermon on the church; greatness in the kingdom, scandal, forgiveness (18:1-35)

V Journey to Jerusalem and Ministry there (19:1-25:46)

(a) Narrative: teaching, rich man, parable of the workers, third passion prediction, healings, entry to Jerusalem and cleansing of Temple, controversies with authorities (19:1-23:39)

(b) Discourse: eschatological sermon, parousia parables (24:1-25:46)

Climax: Passion, Death and Resurrection (26:1-28:20)

(a) Conspiracy against Jesus, Last Supper, agony in garden (26:1-46)

(b) Arrest, trials before Sanhedrin and Pilate, mockery, crucifixion, death (26:47-27:56)

(c) Burial, guard at tomb, empty tomb, bribery of guard, resurrection appearances (27:57-28:20)

STORYLINE

Like the other gospels, Matthew is a narrative. It begins with Jesus' family tree, describes the circumstances of his birth and events in his ministry culminating in his death and resurrection appearances to women and disciples. It is a narrative based on historical happenings that were already shaped into traditions which the author drew on to tell his distinctive story. It is enriched with extensive teachings of Jesus, organised into five imposing discourses aimed at bringing the reader into contact with the power of Jesus' teaching. His frequent use of the Old Testament, concerns for the Law and critique of the Jewish leaders for rejecting Jesus, show that he was steeped in the Jewish heritage. He demonstrates how Jesus fulfils the hopes and dreams of Israel, and how God now extends his offer of salvation to the gentiles as well.

Chapters one and two are somewhat akin to a summary, introducing themes that will be developed in the rest of the story. Jesus' Jewish heritage is highlighted by means of a genealogy. He is 'the son of David, the son of Abraham'. The royal ancestor is mentioned first since this is a lengthy and precise genealogy of who Jesus the Messiah is. He will fulfil the promise to Abraham of being a blessing for the nations. The unusual inclusion of women who served as God's instruments prepares for the unique role of Mary who conceives through the power of the Spirit. A new creative act brings the Messiah into being and relates him uniquely to God, yet he is also a son of David through legal adoption by Joseph.

After the birth of Jesus the pagan magi, guided by revelation in nature and confirmed by the Jewish scriptures, come to pay homage. The Jews, on the other hand, do not believe and Herod even seeks to kill the child. But God frustrates his plan when Joseph takes the family to Egypt and later back to Nazareth. Into this account the evangelist weaves five citations from the prophets that show the Messiah reliving the climactic moments of Israelite history – the exodus and the exile – and thereby identifies him with Israel's struggle for freedom. In this way the infancy narrative is firmly inserted into the Old Testament background and Jesus, the Messiah of David, unique Son of God, Emmanuel, is presented as the climax of Old Testament history and the fulfilment of its prophecy.

The public ministry of Jesus is prepared for by the preaching of John the Baptist as Isaiah had foretold. As Jesus is baptised the Spirit descends and a heavenly voice recognises Jesus as 'my beloved Son'. The three temptation scenes that follow attempt to divert Jesus from his mission by adapting it to worldly standards,

but Jesus, unlike the chosen people in the desert, does not suc-
cumb. He begins his preaching of the kingdom of heaven in
Galilee, fulfilling Isaiah's prophecy. He then summons disciples
and the section ends with a summary of Jesus' ministry of teaching and healing which draws a huge response from broken and
needy people.

The Sermon on the Mount presents Jesus as the authoritative
teacher of God's will in continuity with the Law of Moses that he
now brings to its fullest expression. The beatitudes express values on which Jesus places priority for disciples, who in turn are
to be the salt of the earth and the light of the world. In a series of
antitheses, Jesus extends and deepens the Mosaic Law. He re-
shapes the traditional exercises of Jewish piety by warning
against ostentation and gives the model of prayer, the 'Our
Father'. There is instruction on behaviour for the kingdom; it is
of such a kind that it demands total dedication to God and is
summed up in the golden rule: 'Do to others as you would have
them do to you' (7:12). The sermon ends by cautioning against
the danger of false prophets and praise for those who not only
hear Jesus' teaching, but also put it into practice. The entire sermon illustrates the core spirit of Jesus' teaching and the crowds
are astonished.

In the narrative section that follows, miracle stories are inter-
woven with discipleship stories. They portray Jesus not only as
authoritative in word, but also mighty in deed. The narrator
emphasises the divine power that works through Jesus, thereby
fulfilling the prophetic promise of Isaiah 53:4. The discipleship
stories lay stress on the demands of discipleship; only those
fully committed to following Jesus will be able to withstand encounters with the powers of evil.

The mission discourse is set in the context of the sending out
of the twelve disciples with authority to preach and heal. In its
present form, the discourse can be read on two levels: as part of
Jesus' ministry that was confined to Israel, and as instruction for
the post-Easter church for which it has ongoing relevance. There
are the demands of austerity and a warning of persecution. The

Spirit will enable those on trial to speak boldly, and the discourse continues with a note of encouragement assuring divine care in the midst of division and difficult choices. It ends by assuring that whoever receives missionaries receives Jesus and whoever receives him receives the God who sent him.

In the narrative section, John the Baptist's questions from prison afford the author the opportunity to explain that Jesus is the Messiah prophesied by Isaiah, and that John is the expected Elijah sent to prepare Israel for God's visitation now manifest in Jesus' activity. Jesus sharply criticises his generation for not recognising, much less accepting, John the Baptist or himself. He also addresses prophetic woes to unbelieving cities. Jesus ends by thanking God his Father for the revelation given to little ones and invites those who are heavily laden to seek repose in him. There follows a series of controversies that have christological import in that Jesus claims to be greater than the Temple and Lord of the sabbath, thus prompting the Pharisees to plot his death. Jesus is the healing servant foretold by Isaiah. Controversy with the Pharisees over the source of Jesus' power comes to a close when Jesus designates his true family as those who do the will of God.

The parable discourse contains seven parables that both reveal and conceal the mystery of the kingdom. Unless the listeners are willing to probe beneath the surface like the disciples, the true meaning of the parables will escape them. The triumph of the kingdom in spite of obstacles invites followers to put everything aside and be fully committed. The church, like the world, is a mixture of good and evil that will continue till the judgement.

Jesus' ministry of teaching and healing continues with a new intensity. He turns his attention to his disciples from whom the church will develop, founded on the rock of Peter. After being rejected by his townspeople, the death of John the Baptist and the feeding of the 5000, Jesus walks on the water. The narrator adds a scene in which Jesus invites Peter to come to him on the water. When Peter's courage fails him, Jesus offers a helping

hand. This is the first of three episodes in this section that highlight the role of Peter. Arrived at Genesareth Jesus heals the sick,
multiplies the loaves and engages in a debate with the scribes
and Pharisees over defilement, and hostile confrontations follow.
In contrast, there is the climactic saying of Peter who confesses
Jesus as the Messiah, the Son of the living God. Peter will become the rock on which Christ will build his church against
which demonic powers will not prevail. He is given the keys of
the kingdom and the power to bind and lose. Yet Peter is chast-
ised for his failure to accept the necessity of Jesus' suffering. The
transfiguration scene highlights the divine sonship of Jesus and
the question about Elijah brings the scene to a close as the disciples descend the mountain. The story of the epileptic boy is followed by the second prediction of the passion and a third scene
with Peter, focused on the Temple tax issue.

The discourse on the community is a collection of parables
and sayings addressed to the disciples, but given a perspective
suited to the later church. The call not to seek one's own aggrand-
isement but to care instead for weaker members and not to scan-
dalise nor despise others, is followed by practical procedures
aimed at settling disputes. Christian forgiveness is to imitate the
unlimited range of God's forgiveness and is illustrated by a
parable. The discourse offers a model for the church emphasising the care Christians need to have for each other as followers
of Christ.

The narrative section is mostly directed to the instruction of
the disciples: marriage and divorce, accepting children, the danger of riches, the parable of the workers in the vineyard, the
third passion prediction, the request of the mother of the sons of
Zebedee for the first places in the kingdom, followed by the
healing of two blind men. Jesus enters Jerusalem in triumph,
cleanses the Temple and teaches there, but Jewish authorities
remain hostile. This is a section filled with sharp clashes as the
authority of Jesus is questioned, followed by the parables of the
two sons, the tenants and the wedding feast. There is teaching
on taxes, resurrection, the greatest commandment, and David's

son. The denunciation of the scribes and Pharisees is an attack on their hypocritical behaviour and love of honours. It ends with seven woes against their casuistry and so they become negative examples for disciples. Jesus reflects on the fate of the Temple and the end of history, followed by parables urging disciples to remain watchful. Jesus is portrayed as judge in the final judgement based on the love commandment.

The passion story moves quickly from Jesus' prediction of a plot, through the Last Supper, prayer in the garden and arrest, to interrogation and trial before the Sanhedrin. The betrayal of Judas, his remorse and death are highlighted. This is followed by the trial before Pilate during which Pilate's wife receives a dream revelation that Jesus is a just man. Then there is the crucifixion, mockery and death. The burial and posting of the guard prepare the scene for the resurrection. The narrator stresses that what is happening fulfils the scriptures in harmony with the many fulfilment citations throughout the gospel. Jesus remains the majestic Messiah throughout, has prophetic knowledge of events and is fully aware of his impending death. To the High Priest he calmly predicts his eventual triumph and at death is acclaimed Son of God. For the evangelist, the death of Jesus is the climactic event ushering in the final age of human history. Signs of the new eschatological age are already evident. Not only is the veil of the Temple torn, but apocalyptic signs in nature occur as the earth is shaken, rocks are rent, tombs are opened and the dead appear in Jerusalem after Jesus is raised. The age of the resurrection begins and with it the mission to the gentiles.

In the story of the empty tomb there is an earthquake as an angel descends to roll back the stone and the guards are struck with fear. In response to the angel's message that Jesus has risen, the women run with joy to tell the disciples and Jesus himself appears to them on the way. The guards are bribed by the chief priests to say that the disciples stole the body. There is a final scene on the mountain top when Jesus, as the exalted Lord to whom all power has been given, commissions his followers to make disciples of all the nations, to baptise and instruct them

with the assurance that he will be with them to the end of the
age. This echoes the name Emmanuel, God-with-us, given to
Jesus in 1:23, and forms a fitting closure to the gospel.

JESUS IN MATTHEW'S GOSPEL

The Narrative as a Whole
The gospel of Matthew is more comprehensive than Mark's, yet
it follows Mark's storyline from baptism to tomb and does not
alter his understanding of Jesus. Matthew, however, did not
simply repeat Mark's christology; he edits, expands and adds
new insights. His distinctive contribution is in the addition of
the narrative accounts of the birth and resurrection appearances.
These serve to connect Jesus to the story of Israel and to the life
of the church respectively. Thus the life of Jesus is stretched over
a larger canvas. Matthew adds appearances of the risen Christ to
women returning from the tomb and to disciples on a mountain
in Galilee, where they are commissioned to preach to the whole
world with the assurance that Jesus will be with them. He inserts the risen Jesus into the church built on the rock of Peter. For
Matthew, the church becomes the locus of Jesus' ongoing activity
as risen Lord. Jesus was not only historically at work during his
ministry; as risen Lord, he continues to challenge his community
both by word and example. This ongoing work of Christ is particularly evident in the community discourse (ch 18) which is
shaped with the post-Easter community in mind. In it the presence of Christ who exercises authority in and through the
church is easily recognised: 'For where two or three are gathered
in my name, I am there among them' (18:20). Christ, by his presence, guides his community, the church, until the end of the age
(cf.28:20) when he will come again. The in-between time is one
of expectation and preparation evident in the parousia parables
(24:42-25:30). These are immediately followed by the judgement
scene when Christ will come to judge the nations (25:31-46):
'Thus the picture of Jesus Christ encompasses the Jesus who was

at work on earth, was installed in power at the resurrection, and continues his salvific work in the church.'[14]

Matthew is faithful to the major themes of Mark's christology in presenting Jesus as Messiah, Son of God and Son of Man. Even so, the changes in his narrative profoundly affect his christology. For example, the genealogy of Jesus and the events surrounding his birth enrich Matthew's understanding of Jesus as Messiah and Son of God. The Sermon on the Mount presents Jesus as an authoritative interpreter of the will of God, the teacher of righteousness par excellence. The gospel ends with the abiding presence of Jesus with his church.

In focusing on Jesus' ancestry, birth, baptism and temptation scenes, Matthew presents a clear portrait of Jesus' identity for the reader before describing his ministry to Israel. Jesus is the Davidic Messiah, Son of God, Emmanuel who embodies the hopes and aspirations of his people. Why? Because he is conceived from the Holy Spirit and so he has a unique relationship to God. His birth is the fulfilment of prophecy, his mission is to save his people from their sins as the name 'Jesus' indicates. Jesus is the presence of God with his people. As messianic Son of God he relives the climactic moments in the history of his people. Matthew employs a series of quotations to show that the events of Jesus' infancy fulfil the scriptures. He is born of a virgin as prophesied by Isaiah, he is born in Bethlehem according to Micah, his return from Egypt fulfils the prophecy of Hosea, and Herod's massacre of the infants fulfils the words of Jeremiah. The appearance of Jesus is therefore in accordance with God's plan as revealed in the scriptures. Matthew then gives us an important insight into Jesus' sonship in the temptation scenes. In them Jesus demonstrates that he is God's Son by his obedience to God's will.

Thus right from the beginning of his gospel, Matthew presents his readers with a rich christology. Jesus is the messianic Son of David, son of Abraham. He is therefore the legitimate King of the Jews who will shepherd God's people. Conceived

14. R. Schnackenburg, ibid, p 83

through the power of the Spirit, he is the beloved Son of God who also embodies the history of his people and fulfils its scriptures. His mission is to save his people from their sins through his obedient response to God, his Father. He is Emmanuel, the one in whom God is present to his people.

Matthew goes on to present Jesus, the messianic Son of God, proclaiming the kingdom of heaven, i.e. God's coming in power to exercise his rule over all. In the gospel there are more than ninety references to the kingdom of God and its equivalents, the majority of which are located in the five discourses. Matthew therefore wishes to lay special emphasis on Jesus' preaching of the 'gospel of the kingdom' which is evident also in key summaries (4:23, 9:35). Jesus' inaugural proclamation (4:17) shows that the future kingdom is already in some sense present when God draws near in his Son to teach and heal every disease and infirmity amongst the people. Certain parables imply that the growth in the kingdom is the result of small beginnings (13:33), a growth that continues in the church (13:32). A number of sayings extend the kingdom into the future (5:19, 6:10, 7:21, etc), and are associated with the Son of Man (13:36-43) and the last judgement (25:31-46). There are also kingdom sayings with ethical implications: only those who bear fruit (7:16, 20) will be permitted to enter. This fruit is measured by the standard of righteousness, embodied and taught by Jesus. The kingdom of God is also opposed by the kingdom of Satan, an opposition highlighted by the continuous battle between Jesus and Satan (cf 12:22-38).

The kingdom of heaven is the message of Jesus, but also the message about Jesus proclaimed in the church. It is anticipated in the present and grows mysteriously. It is present in the Christian community, but the church is not yet the kingdom which is primarily eschatological. Yet in the present it draws near with Jesus as inaugurator and model. The prerequisites for entering the kingdom are ethical and moral, the believer must endeavour to bear fruit by righteous living. The apocalyptic events surrounding the death and resurrection of Jesus open up a new stage in the establishment of the kingdom since the exalted Christ already has total power over the cosmos (28:18). His return at the end of time will mean the final and definitive establishment of God's kingdom (16:27-28). In the meantime, the church is the instrument of the kingdom in the present age, but not co-terminus with it; it is a place where Jesus is confessed, worshipped and obeyed. Making disciples of all the nations is the mission of the church as it journeys through history towards the consummation of the kingdom.

In the Sermon on the Mount Jesus, as one who enjoys intimate knowledge of God's will, proclaims the kingdom by teaching his disciples how to practise a greater righteousness, thereby fulfilling the Law and the prophets. Jesus' healing ministry fulfils the prophecy of Isaiah (53:4). The mighty deeds of Jesus further disclose the identity of Jesus' person, whose deeds are works of the Messiah no less (cf 11:2). In the mission discourse, Jesus makes statements that point to his own unique relationship with God (10:32-33). Yet the Messiah's ministry of preaching, teaching and healing does not lead Israel to repentance. In the midst of opposition from Jewish leaders, Matthew provides important christological statements in disclosing the intimate relationship that the Son enjoys with the Father (11:25-27). When Jesus withdraws because of the Pharisees' plottings, Matthew introduces and extends the quote from Isaiah 42:1-4 (12:18-21). Jesus is the chosen Servant of God to proclaim justice to the nations.

Jesus delivers a discourse in parables, in which he reveals the mysteries of the kingdom to his disciples. The parable of the weeds and its explanation (13:24-30, 36-43) provides a new insight into Matthew's christology. The one who sows the good seed is the Son of Man, the enemy who sows the weeds is the devil. At the present time they continue to grow side by side, but at the end of the ages the Son of Man will send his angels to separate the two and the righteous will shine in the kingdom of the Father. Matthew feels no need to explain who the Son of Man is, for readers know that he is Jesus, the Son of Man who will return again.

In one major respect Matthew differs from Mark. In the latter
no human character recognises Jesus as Son of God until after
his death (Mk 15:39). In Matthew, the disciples confess Jesus as
Son of God (cf 14:33, 16:17). They may not understand its full
significance during his ministry, but they already recognise the
one who preaches, teaches and heals in the service of the kingdom as having a unique relationship to God. Jesus explains to
them (16:21) that the Son of Man must suffer, die and be raised.
In addition, Jesus identifies himself as the Son of Man who will
come 'with his angels in the glory of his Father' (16:27). Son of
Man is the distinctive way Jesus refers to himself in connection
with his destiny, identifying himself as God's eschatological
judge. Jesus' use of the term clarifies his messianic destiny as
one who will suffer, die, rise and return again. From the perspective of the resurrection, believers identify Jesus as the Son of
Man who is also Messiah and Son of God.

Matthew portrays Jesus' entry into Jerusalem (21:1-11) in a
manner at odds with conventional Jewish messianic expectation. He enters as a meek and humble king foretold in Zechariah
9:9. He will not be a powerful warrior king, but a servant king
who will save his people from their sins by giving his life on
their behalf (26:28). People in need recognise who Jesus is and
address him as Son of David, while religious leaders do not.
Jesus is the son sent by the owner of the vineyard and since the
tenants refuse to accept him, cast him out and kill him, the kingdom of God will be taken from Israel and given to a people that
will bear fruit (21:23-43). Jesus is the son for whom the king has
prepared a wedding feast, but because those invited refused to
come, the invitation is now extended to others (22:1-14).

In the final discourse, Jesus looks to the future and instructs
his followers on how to conduct themselves as they await the
parousia of the Son of Man. He will come in a way that no one
can mistake – on the clouds of heaven with power and glory to
gather his elect (24:29-31). Accompanied by his angels and seated
on his throne, he will judge the nations (25:31-46). Jesus then as-
cribes a glorious future to himself as God's eschatological judge

acting with God's power and authority. Before all this takes place, however, the Son of Man must first obediently surrender his life on the cross.

Matthew's passion narrative portrays Jesus as the obedient Son of God who pours out his life for the forgiveness of sins. Before the Sanhedrin, while not denying that he is the Messiah and Son of God, Jesus prophecies that he will return as Son of Man on the clouds of heaven. At his death apocalyptic signs occur leading the pagan centurion and those with him to acknowledge Jesus as Son of God (27:51-54). These signs surrounding the confession are dramatic and clearly indicate that the time of the gentiles has begun.

The resurrection is God's vindication of Jesus' obedient death. The risen Lord instructs the women to tell the disciples that he will meet them in Galilee. As the disciples worship their Lord, the narrative is brought to a close in such a way that makes for a new beginning. The time of the mission to Israel is concluded and the church's universal mission is about to begin. Jesus the Messiah inaugurated the kingdom of heaven by his ministry and death on the cross. Now as risen Lord he sends his followers to make disciples of all the nations with the assurance of his presence, as they await the return of the Son of Man who will gather his elect and judge the nations.

Titles of Jesus

Matthew's narrative christology follows, as we have seen, the main overall structure of Mark's, yet he edits his material carefully to present a distinctive image of Jesus. In this picture, traditional titles acquire new accents and emphases, and other titles become prominent.[15] In the opening chapters Matthew relates that Jesus is the promised Messiah sent to renew Israel; the Son of God who enjoys familiarity with the Father and reveals his will; the Son of Man who suffers rejection, yet will judge the nations at the end of time; the Saviour who takes away our sins revealed in the name 'Jesus'; the authoritative Teacher surpassing

15. Cf R. Schnackenburg, ibid, pp 96-130

Moses whose interpretation of the Law brings to fulfilment its
God-given purpose; the compassionate Son of David who heals
human infirmity; Emmanuel, or God-with-us, who will abide
with his community as Lord of the church till the end of the age.
Because Jesus is the promised Messiah, Matthew reads the history
of the Jews and their scriptures as finding ultimate meaning in
Jesus. This explains his extensive use of the Old Testament, especially his fulfilment quotations, to demonstrate that Jesus'
mission is in full harmony with the will of God expressed in the
scriptures.

Son of God. All the christological titles in Matthew culminate
in Jesus as Son of God. He has kept Mark's baptismal scene, the
transfiguration, Jesus before the Sanhedrin and the centurion's
confession of faith. But Matthew tells us that Jesus is also born of
the virgin Mary, having been conceived by the Holy Spirit (1:20).
That is, his true origin is in God and so he is called Emmanuel or
God-with-us (1:23). He is adored by the magi (2:11) and fulfils
Hosea's prophecy as 'my Son' (2:15). The Father himself identifies Jesus as his beloved Son in whom he is well pleased (3:17,
17:5). In the temptation scene he is challenged by the devil with
regard to his divine sonship: 'If you are the Son of God …' (4:3,
6). He teaches the crowds as one having authority from God (e.g.
7:29). It is as Son of God that he heals, walks on the water, rescues Peter from the waves and elicits from the disciples the confession: 'Truly you are the Son of God' (14:33). Peter declares
him to be 'The Messiah, the Son of the living God' (16:16). The
disciples have already begun to recognise Jesus' unique relationship to God, even if they do not fully comprehend its full
implications. The earthly Jesus is recognised by the demons as
Son of God who stands in close proximity to God. He is the Son
who perfectly fulfils all righteousness demanded by the will of
God (3:13-15), and so he is able to proclaim God's will in word
and deed while remaining obedient to the end.

This close connection with God finds clear expression in
11:27: 'All things have been handed over to me by my Father;
and no one knows the Son except the Father, and no one knows

the Father except the Son and anyone to whom the Son chooses to reveal him.' There is mutual knowledge between Father and Son that enables the Son to convey knowledge of the Father to others. Jesus has authority to reveal and save because of the loving familiarity existing between him and his Father. There follows the invitation of Jesus to take his yoke and accept his teaching and thus find rest. This is an extended view of the Markan Son of God. Jesus' answer to the High Priest, though, is more reserved (cf 26:63-64). He is mocked on the cross as the Son of God (27:40, 43), and breathes his last while trusting in God's faithfulness (27:50). Special events occur after his death – the Temple curtain is rent, there is an earthquake, rocks are split, tombs are opened and the centurion and his soldiers confess Jesus as Son of God. In this way the power of the Son of God reveals itself in death and is confirmed by the gospel's closing scene. The disciples are to baptise in the name of the Father and of the Son and of the Holy Spirit (28:20). The mockery of Jesus as Son of God at the crucifixion is now fully vindicated by God. For those who believe, Jesus, the Son of God, becomes 'God-with-us', present in the midst of his community (18:20) to guide and protect believers until the end of time. Living in closest communion with the Father, he carries on the work of salvation in his church through word and sacrament (cf 28:18-20).

Son of Man. While the Son of God is a more comprehensive title for Matthew, the Son of Man title occurs some thirty times throughout the narrative with a range and depth of meaning. As Son of Man, Jesus is the humble servant during the public ministry yet possesses divine forgiveness. He is the friend of sinners and Lord of the sabbath. He is the suffering, dying and rising servant, Lord of the universe, and judge on the last day when he comes in glory accompanied by his angels. The title is taken over from Mark, but also from the 'sayings' source (Q). There are ten additional passages in Matthew in which the powerful appearance of the Son of Man dominates. This earthly activity of the Son of Man is oriented towards the harvest at the end of time (cf 13:40-42).

The whole world and all the nations will be subject to the demands of the Son of Man to whom all authority in heaven and earth has been given. By his death and resurrection, Jesus has been exalted to God's right hand. Thus the prophecy of Daniel 7:13-14 and the declaration of Jesus in 26:64 are both fulfilled as the risen Jesus comes to his church to remain with it until the end of time (28:18-20). Jesus is definitively exalted to become ruler of the universe and of his church. He summons his followers to make disciples, to baptise and to teach all that he has taught them. Here is the founding of the church with its world-embracing scope, new initiation rite and new Law. Thus christology is at the basis of the church's existence and activity. This Emmanuel (1:23) who promised to be in the midst of his disciples gathered in his name (18:20), now promises a universal presence in his worldwide church throughout the whole of history until he comes to judge the nations. The church is thus sustained by his energising presence empowering it for mission.

Messiah. Matthew's distinctive portrayal of Jesus comes through his use of two titles in particular: Jesus as Messiah and Son of David. In doing so he connects Jesus more directly to traditional messianic expectations within Judaism already present in Mark. Matthew extends this usage. His designation of Jesus as Son of David is limited to his earthly activity amongst the people of Israel. Since Jesus is the long-awaited Messiah, Matthew begins his narrative with a detailed genealogy to portray Jesus, the Messiah, as the culmination of Israel's history. Although conceived through the Holy Spirit, he is a descendant of David through legal adoption by Joseph. He is born in David's city, Bethlehem, as the prophet foretold. This Son of David changes and surpasses the hopes of Israel. He comes to inaugurate the kingdom of heaven in opposition to Satan's rule through his preaching, teaching and healing ministry, all of which promote the in-breaking of God's rule. He comes to take the infirmities of the people on himself (8:16-17). He enters the royal city not as a conqueror, but as a humble king (21:5) to bring peace. It is the 'nobodies' of society who acknowledge him as Son of David.

Because of his Jewish background and that of part of his audience, Matthew holds on to the title Son of David and uses it as a point of departure for his delineation of the Christian Messiah. For him, Jesus is more than the Son of David, he is also the Son of God. Related to the Son of David and Messiah are King of the Jews, King of Israel, Lord and 'Jesus Christ' (the anointed one, Messiah) actually becames the set designation for the unique figure of Jesus of Nazareth. In him the hopes of Israel are fulfilled as the expected Messiah, but he surpasses even the wildest of Jewish expectations: 'You are the Messiah, the Son of the living God' (16:16, cf 16:20). He will not be a political liberator, but, as his name Jesus designates, he will free his people from their sins (1:21).

Teacher. Although he is called teacher proportionately less often than in Mark, Jesus' most prominent activity in Matthew is teaching. The very structure of the gospel makes it clear that Jesus is a teacher. In Mark, Matthew found only two lengthy discourses (chs 4, 13). He expands the discourse material to the point that the placement of it becomes a key structural element in his gospel narrative. The whole public ministry of Jesus is divided into narratives followed by five lengthy discourses addressed to the disciples and, in part, to the crowds. Each discourse is clearly marked off with a concluding formula (7:28, 11:1, 13:53, 19:1, 26:1). The narrative material preceding each of the discourses prepares for the ensuing discourse. What Jesus teaches (4:23) is the content of the five discourses in Matthew. It is to this teaching that the risen Jesus refers to in 28:20.

From the beginning of his public ministry, Matthew focuses on the teaching of Jesus and gives examples that fit the narrative context. After the parable discourse in chapter thirteen, Jesus devotes himself more and more to the instruction of his disciples, the nucleus of the future church. Furthermore, in addition to the five lengthy discourses, the teaching of Jesus is evident from different pericopes scattered throughout the gospel, e.g. sabbath controversies, laws of ritual cleanliness, rejection of the Pharisees' teaching. It is clear then that the teaching of Jesus has been deliberately highlighted by Matthew as he reconstructs the framework of Mark. Jesus becomes the sole teacher for Christians: 'One is your teacher ... your instructor is one, the Messiah' (23:8,10). Yet paradoxically, the disciples never address him as teacher. This form of address is confined to unbelievers or those not fully committed to following him. Since they only recognise him as a human teacher, this title is clearly inadequate for someone who possesses divine authority over the letter of the Mosaic Law. What is lacking in such people is the insight of faith, that understanding which, unlike Mark, Matthew is willing to attribute to the disciples during the public ministry. Jesus' parables are perfectly intelligible to the disciples who 'see and hear' (13:16-17). Since Jesus' presence in the church is mediated by his words, it is essential that those who hear them in faith fully understand so that they can pass them on to others.

One of the eschatological functions given to Jesus in Matthew is the interpretation of the Torah expressed programatically in the Sermon on the Mount. Jesus reveals the full meaning of the Torah that is the expression of God's will. In 5:17-20 he enunciates what he will fill out with concrete examples (5:21-48). Jesus' attitude to the Law and the prophets is not one of annulment, but of bringing them to eschatological fulfilment, a prophetic fulfilment that even rescinds the letter of the Law to complete its meaning. The disciples who are intent on doing God's will must transcend the casuistry of the Pharisees, the letter must give way to the definitive teaching of Jesus. This radicalisation of the Law is grounded christologically.

In the antitheses on murder, adultery and love, Jesus radicalises the Law by extending and interiorising the obligation; for divorce, oaths and retaliation, he abrogates the letter of the Law. In each case, it is the word of Jesus that decides the issue: '... but I say to you ...' His words are on a par with those spoken by God to Moses, but Jesus requires a righteousness that transcends the demands of the Law. By teaching a superior way of righteousness, Jesus demonstrates that he has an understanding of God's will that is accessible only to God's Messiah. His teaching is therefore implicitly christological.

Another feature discernible in Jesus' teaching is a love for people because of the love he has received from God. Matthew's emphasis on love and mercy is evident in special sayings and special passages, e.g. 'Go and learn what this means, "I desire mercy, and not sacrifice".' 'For I have come to call not the righteous, but sinners' (9:13; cf 12:7). The showing of mercy appropriate to the mercy experienced from God becomes the criterion of concrete action as the parable of the unforgiving servant demonstrates (18:23-35). In the last judgement scene, concrete works of love to those in need exemplify the mercy that is expected of disciples (25:31-46). In Matthew's gospel, Jesus is the one who presents the love and mercy of God in his person and in his words and deeds. In turn, he requires works of love as the concrete expression of the new and greater righteousness. The love of neighbour is placed on the same level as the love of God (cf 22:37-40).

Lord of the Church. Matthew alone uses the word 'church' (16:18, 18:17) in his gospel. Despite its infrequent use, the whole public ministry of Jesus aims at gathering disciples into the embryonic church (21:43). Since Israel disowns its Messiah (27:25), the kingdom is now transferred to the church. All the discourses, especially the one on order in the church (ch 18), contain directions for disciples living in the church. It is made up of those who heed Jesus' call to follow him with total commitment (cf 4:18-22). Unlike the disciples in Mark, they believe (14:33) and understand (13:51), yet faced with a crisis they panic, and act as if they have no faith (cf 'little faith', 8:26, 14:31, 17:20). Nevertheless, they do accept the teaching of Jesus and obey it. Such obedient action makes the disciples brothers and sisters of Jesus in the family of God. This 'righteousness' focuses on the essential elements of loving God and neighbour (22:34-40) and Jesus himself becomes the ultimate norm of morality for the disciple both by word and example, since Jesus is the prime example of an obedient Son (4:1-11).

Matthew treats the disciples more formally than Mark does for they represent, not all the followers of Jesus, but specifically the Twelve chosen to hand on his teachings to the world (cf 28:20). To accomplish this, they must understand the mysteries of the kingdom. They see and hear what others do not (13:10-17), they understand all things taught by Jesus and are therefore 'scribes educated for the kingdom of heaven' (13:51-52). Yet Matthew does not gloss over their failures: Judas betrays him, Peter denies him, all abandon him, even at the appearance of the risen Lord 'some doubted.' They are people of 'little faith.' Matthew singles out Peter as representative of the disciples. He is invited to walk on the water (14:28 ff), recognises Jesus' identity (16:16) to which Jesus responds by offering him a position of authority in the church, and he is invited to pay the Temple tax 'for me and for you' (17:24-27).

A Jewish-Christian and a gentile-Christian perspective is detectable in Matthew. He holds on to the former: Jesus was sent to Israel, fulfils the Law, uses the Jewish concepts of the kingdom of heaven and righteousness, and mentions that Jesus is a descendent from David. Other passages betray an anti-Jewish polemic: Jesus' rejection of Jewish legalism and his blistering attack on the scribes and Pharisees. On the other hand, there is the gathering of the community of salvation when the risen Christ sends out his disciples to the whole world. All this has consequences for Matthew's picture of Jesus Christ. Jesus emerges from Judaism and remains connected with it. He is the son of David and upholds the Law even when he interprets it in a new way. He retains the Jewish practices of piety (6:1-18) and Peter pays the Temple tax for both of them. The Son of God is the Jewish Messiah (26:63-64) and is condemned as King of the Jews (27:37). The Old Testament people of God, in the church community, have become the true Israel capable of producing fruit.

The gospel is therefore a presentation developed from the early Jewish-Christian community, but also addressed to non-Jewish Christians. It is interesting also that the pagan magi pay homage to the infant Jesus. Jesus begins his ministry in Galilee of the gentiles and he heals the servant of the pagan centurion who is praised for his faith (cf 8:5-13). Although Jesus' ministry is largely to Israel, he wanders into pagan territory to encounter a Canaanite woman whose daughter he cures because of her great faith (15:21-28). The gentile mission is foreshadowed by the parable of the wedding banquet when the servants go out to invite anyone they meet (22:1-14). The good news is to be preached throughout the world (24:14), the judgement of the nations affects everyone, and the risen Christ appears in Galilee to commission his followers. Matthew has juxtaposed the 'sending' to the lost sheep of the house of Israel during Jesus' ministry with the commission of the risen Christ to all nations. Here the historical situation in the time of Jesus is transparent for the future mission (cf 10:1-42). Jesus' instructions to the disciples whom he sends to Israel retain their validity for the post-Easter church.

Fulfils the Scriptures. Matthew sees Jesus as the fulfilment of Old Testament prophecies and promises, but he does so from a Jewish-Christian perspective. He adopts prophecies and fits them into a post-Easter view much more that Mark does. The whole gospel is filled with quotations and allusions to the word of God in the Old Testament. In this way the picture of Jesus, through its connection with the Jewish scriptures, turns into a faith picture of Jesus Christ. The life and mission of Jesus is seen as predestined by God.

Matthew sees the origin and birth of Jesus descending from the people of Abraham. It is also clear from the genealogy that he is a son of David. To this is appended Isaiah 7:14 which focuses on Jesus as Emmanuel (1:23). The birth in Bethlehem is foretold in Micah and together with three other fulfilment quotes shows that the childhood of Jesus is attested in the scriptures. At the beginning of the proclamation in Galilee of the gentiles (4:12-16) Jesus fulfils Isaiah 8:23-9:1, and this serves as a preview of the post-Easter conversion of the gentiles. The words and deeds of Jesus prompt a question from John the Baptist as to whether Jesus is the One to come (11:2-3), and this is answered by Jesus from Isaiah. With the growing resistance to and rejection of Jesus, the fulfilment of Isaiah 42:1-4 acquires special significance

(12:18-21). The split between disciples and opponents highlights the fulfilment of Isaiah 6:9-10 (13:14-15). A turning point occurs at Caesarea Philippi when Jesus reveals to his disciples his way of suffering and death. However, it is not until he enters Jerusalem (21:1-5) that there are fulfilment quotations from Isaiah 62:11 and Zechariah 9:9. A final complex of fulfilment quotations is gathered in the passion story. Jesus is arrested in accordance with the scriptures, he is betrayed for thirty pieces of silver, given vinegar to drink, has his clothes divided, is mocked and prays as he breathes his last. Here Matthew is largely following Mark. In his suffering and death Jesus understands that it is in keeping with the will of God attested in the scriptures. So then Jesus' entire journey is a chain of fulfilled promises. In this way the story of Jesus is inserted into a story of salvation that incorporates the Christ event into the history of Israel and lifts it to a higher key. What the scriptures have proclaimed must now be seen in a new light.

What is significant about the fulfilment quotations, which are usually introduced by 'to fulfil what had been spoken ...' or similar expressions, is their christological purpose to show Jesus' divine origin from God and his divine status. All Jesus' activity is seen as being under the guidance of God, a compassionate healer whose unobtrusive work brings about the salvation of God. The quotations trace a picture of Jesus in which even the details of his life are interpreted in the light of scripture. From these we learn that Jesus is Emmanuel (Is 7:14), God's Son (Hos 11:1), born in Bethlehem as ruler of God's people (Mic 5:2), his kingship stands out at the entry to Jerusalem (Zec 9:9), he is God's chosen servant who bears the burdens of others (Is 53:4), he speaks in parables (Ps 78:2), is betrayed by a companion (Jer 18:1-3), will proclaim justice to the nations (Is 42:1-4) because in Galilee of the gentiles a light has dawned (Is 9:1-2). Thus Matthew builds a bridge between the Old Testament and the Christ event. Nevertheless, he paints an image of Christ that stands in contrast to the Jewish image of the Messiah. What is new is that the bringer of salvation achieves his goal, not through military conquest or political rule, but through his vicarious atoning death for sinners. Matthew interprets this death in the light of the suffering servant of Isaiah (52:11-53:12). This new understanding of what is meant by saviour and what salvation entails is arrived at from a consideration of the words and deeds of Jesus himself. These show the mercy of God to be the foundation of the salvation event. However, the old people of God through their failure to accept Jesus have lost their privileged position, and now the kingdom of God is handed over to others who will be more responsive. This interpretation of Matthew finds a solid and sure foundation in the scriptures.

The picture of Jesus revealed in the gospel narrative is of one sent by God to be active in Israel, proclaiming salvation to the Jews. There is, however, much more; there emerges the bringer of salvation for the whole world. His missionary mandate at the end of the gospel is of paramount importance for the ongoing life of the church. The kingdom of heaven, first offered to Israel but rejected by its leaders, passes to a new people, and so the history of salvation lives on in the person of the risen Jesus present in the community called together by him. He is Emmanuel, God-with-us, who will abide with his community till the end of the age, when he will lead his people out of history into eternity.

CHAPTER FOUR

The Gospel of Luke

INTRODUCTION

The gospel of Luke is part of a two-volume work, Luke-Acts, that, in the opinion of almost all contemporary scholars, was originally composed as one literary work, and separated in the second century. Each of the two volumes is introduced by a prologue addressed to the same reader, Theophilus (Lk 1:1-4; Acts 1:1-2). The gospel generally follows Mark's basic narrative and also his portrait of Jesus. But Luke extends these by the addition of the infancy narratives and the resurrection appearances. He incorporates extensive material from the 'sayings' source (Q), together with distinctive Lukan material (Special Luke) that gives us such unforgettable parables as the Good Samaritan, the Prodigal Son, the Rich Man and Lazarus, as well as stories of the raising of the widow's son, the healing of the ten lepers and Zacchaeus. These he distributes throughout his story, especially in the 'journey' narrative. Unlike Matthew, who inserts blocks of discourse material into his narrative, Luke interweaves the deeds and sayings of Jesus. He transposes and expands the Nazareth scene (Lk 4:16-30) making it programmatic for Jesus' ministry as a whole. He omits Mk 6:45-8:26, 9:41-10:12 and inserts Lk 6:20-8:3, together with a lengthy travel account (Lk 9:51-19:27) into the Markan sequence. The overall picture gives the impression of Luke's concern to move Jesus to Jerusalem, the city of his destiny. Luke's addition of resurrection appearances in Jerusalem and Jesus' final commissioning before ascending into heaven provide a fitting conclusion to his narrative as well as being a bridge to his second volume. The Acts of the Apostles deals with the birth and expansion of the church in which the exalted Christ is also present through his Spirit. In this way, Luke demonstrates that the church of his day, with the inclusion of the gentiles as part of God's people, fulfils God's promises of old and so confirms his fidelity towards his people (cf Lk 1:4).

From the end of the second century, Luke-Acts has been attributed to Luke, the companion of Paul (cf Col 4:14; 2 Tim 4:11). The author of the two-volume work was certainly not an eyewitness of Jesus' ministry, but a second or third generation Christian who depended on oral and written accounts from those who may have seen or indeed heard Jesus (cf Lk 1:1-3). He wrote a 'narrative account' that is thorough, accurate and orderly, and improves the Greek of Mark. From a study of his work we get the impression that Luke was a gentile convert, well educated in Hellenistic literary techniques and acquainted with Old Testament literary traditions. He is a great storyteller and this enables him to make the account of Jesus and the beginning of the church into a coherent, interconnected narrative. His substitution of Greek names for Hebrew ones, his less than adequate knowledge of Palestinian geography, customs and practices, suggests that he was a non-Palestinian writing for a largely gentile-Christian audience, probably in Greece, but one that was sufficiently steeped in the Old Testament to grasp his allusions. Such a lengthy literary work would probably have been addressed to a wide audience to describe the origin and development of the Christian movement. Luke succeeds in connecting Christians of his generation not only to the early days of the church and to the ministry of Jesus, but also to the whole story of God's people.

Luke's decision to tell his story in a historical sequence affects his portrayal of Jesus. Whereas, in Mark and Matthew, the post-resurrection perspective of the evangelists is implicitly expressed within their narratives of Jesus' ministry, Luke, on the other hand, is able to give full attention to the implications of the resurrection and the sending of the Spirit in a separate volume. His work presents the identity and mission of Jesus in stages that allow a fuller expression of Jesus' humanity within the gospel. He highlights the mercy and compassion of Jesus and has been described as 'the scribe of the gentleness of Christ.' The work begun by Jesus continues in his church through specially chosen witnesses who were prepared by him during his historical ministry and were commissioned after his resurrection. In Acts, Luke provides a broad survey of how the church developed and expanded from Jerusalem to the ends of the earth (cf Acts 1:8). The story begun in Jesus' lifetime continues through specific people under the Spirit's guidance. Any discussion of Luke's christology, therefore, must be conscious of the literary unity of Luke-Acts.

Luke is also anxious to anchor the Jesus story and its sequel in history by relating it to people, times and epochs. Jesus' life is set in the framework of a story that is related to the Roman world of the time (Lk 2:1-2, 3:1; Acts 11:28, 18:2, 12, 25:11). Luke's story is also related to Palestinian history both secular and religious (1:5, 3:1-2). He alone has written a sequel to the Jesus story by relating the emergence of the church, thereby tying the Jesus event to church history as well. However, this historical concern on the part of Luke is part of a larger theological concern, that is, salvation history. Jesus comes at the end of one historical period and at the beginning of another, and this is all part of God's plan to save human beings that was initiated during the Old Testament period. Jesus fulfils the plan of God: 'events that have been fulfilled among us' (1:1). Luke alone, among the synoptic writers, calls Jesus 'Saviour' (2:11), and writes from the perspective of the church towards the end of the first century. He divides salvation history into the period of Israel (cf 16:16); the period of Jesus' ministry, death and exaltation (3:2-24:51) when salvation was accomplished; the period of the church from Jesus' ascension and the coming of the Spirit to the parousia during which salvation is extended to the gentiles, thus fulfilling the promise to Abraham (Acts).

Although the basic structure of the gospel narrative is Markan, with one journey to Jerusalem, Luke has enhanced the geographical perspective of Luke-Acts by highlighting the central place Jerusalem holds in his overall work. Jerusalem is the city of destiny for Jesus and the place from which God's word of salvation spreads to the ends of the earth. It is the city of David's throne (cf 1:32-33) and contains the Temple of the Lord. Luke depicts Jesus as making his way to Jerusalem, the place where salvation is to be accomplished. The gospel begins and ends in Jerusalem and in the Temple (1:5ff, 24:53). This also accounts for the reordering of the temptation scenes with the climactic ending on the pinnacle of the Temple (4:1-13). There is a threefold geographical distribution of Jesus' ministry: in Galilee (4:14-9:50), the journey to Jerusalem (9:51-19:27), and the Jerusalem ministry (19:28-21:38). Luke's concern was to move Jesus from Galilee to Jerusalem and Jesus' geographical movements point to his theological concerns. For this purpose he omits Mark 6:45-8:26 that relates Jesus' activity outside of Galilee and introduces Jesus as starting out from Galilee with a solemn announcement (9:51). Three times during the journey specific reference is made to Jerusalem (9:51-53, 13:22, 17:11). Jesus converses with Moses and Elijah about his *exodos*, his departure, that he is to complete in Jerusalem (9:31), his passion, death, resurrection and ascension. Arriving at the city, Jesus enters in triumph seated on a colt and is hailed as king by the crowds thus making it a royal entrance (19:35-38). He goes immediately to the Temple to purify his Father's house. All the post-resurrection appearances take place in the vicinity of Jerusalem, from which place he also ascends to heaven. So it is fitting that it is from Jerusalem that the gospel will spread to the ends of the earth. The following outline and storyline of the gospel will help to see how Luke develops his story and his distinctive portrait of Jesus Christ.

OUTLINE

Prologue (1:1-4)
I The Infancy and Boyhood of Jesus (1:5-2:52)
(a) Annunciations and conceptions of John the Baptist and Jesus: announcements of the births of John and Jesus, visitation, Magnificat (1:5-56)
(b) Birth, circumcision and naming of John and Jesus, birth of

John, Benedictus, birth of Jesus, visit by shepherds, circumcision and naming, presentation in the Temple, return to Nazareth (1:57-2:40)

(c) Jesus in the Temple (2:41-52)

II Preparation for Public Ministry (3:1-4:13)

(a) Preaching of John, baptism of Jesus (3:1-22)

(b) Genealogy of Jesus, temptations (3:23-4:13)

III Ministry in Galilee (4:14-9:50)

(a) Rejection at Nazareth, ministry at Capernaum and by the lake (4:14-5:16)

(b) Healing of paralytic, call of Levi, debates with Pharisees, call of the Twelve, Sermon on the Plain (5:17-6:49)

(c) Healing of centurion's servant, raising of widow's son, Jesus and John, pardon of sinful woman, female followers of Jesus, parables, Jesus' family, calming of the storm, healings, mission of the Twelve (7:1-9:6)

(d) Herod's opinion, feeding of 5000, Peter's confession, first passion prediction and conditions of discipleship, transfiguration, healing of boy, second passion prediction, the greatest in the kingdom (9:7-50)

IV Journey to Jerusalem (9:51-19:27)

(a) First Section: Samaritan inhospitality, followers of Jesus, mission of 72, reproaches on unrepentant cities, praise of the Father, the greatest commandment, Good Samaritan, Martha and Mary, teachings on prayer, Jesus and Beelzebul, denunciation of scribes and Pharisees, persecution, parable of rich fool, providence and vigilance, Jesus a cause of division, need for repentance, parables and cure of crippled woman (9:51-13:21)

(b) Second Section: sayings and parables of lost sheep, lost coin, lost son, dishonest steward, rich man and Lazarus, various sayings (13:22-17:10)

(c) Third Section: ten lepers, coming of Son of Man, persistent widow, Pharisee and tax collector, riches, third passion prediction, healing of blind beggar, Zacchaeus, parable of the coins (17:11-19:27)

V Ministry in Jerusalem (19:28-21:38)

(a) Entry to Jerusalem, cleansing of Temple, controversy with authorities, parable of tenants, taxes, resurrection, David's Son, scribes denounced, widow's coin (19:28-21:4)

(b) Destruction of the Temple and signs of the end (21:5-38)

VI Last Supper, Passion, Death, Burial (21:5-23:56)

(a) Conspiracy, Last Supper (22:1-38)

(b) Agony, arrest, Peter's denial, Jewish and Roman trials (22:39-23:25)

(c) Way of the cross, crucifixion, burial (23:26-56)

VII Resurrection Appearances (24:1-53)

(a) At the empty tomb (24:1-12)

(b) On the road to Emmaus (24:13-35)

(c) In Jerusalem and ascension (24;35-53)

STORYLINE

Luke begins his gospel with an elegant prologue (1:1-4) in which he expounds the reliability of the Christian message that the church in his day proclaimed. The manner in which he has ordered events in his story produces a new narrative. In the infancy account, a transition from the Old Testament to Jesus is effected when representatives of the best in Israelite piety meet the gospel characters of Mary and Jesus, thus demonstrating continuity in God's plan of salvation. The infancy narratives are built on parallels between the conceptions and births of John the Baptist and Jesus, but in each case, Jesus is the greater. The successive episodes are sprinkled with canticles which are a mosaic of Old Testament expressions and allusions. John the Baptist will play the role of Elijah sent to prepare for the Day of the Lord now associated with the coming of Jesus.

Jesus is conceived, not by human generation, but by the creative Spirit of God. The child will not only be the Davidic Messiah, but the Son of God, and Mary responds in obedience. Jesus is fully human, but not an ordinary human being. He is born of the virgin Mary whose virginity is essential to the claim that Jesus is both God's Son and Son of David, Messiah and Lord. She visits Elizabeth and utters the *Magnificat*. Elizabeth gives birth to a son whom she names John, and Zechariah recovers his speech to extol the fulfilment of all that God has promised to Israel in the *Benedictus*. The birth of Jesus is set in a worldwide context to highlight its importance. Angels sing their hymn and shepherds offer homage. Jesus' parents fulfil the Law and Simeon and Anna, representatives of Jewish piety, greet the child Jesus. At the age of twelve, Jesus speaks for the first time in his Father's Temple.

The beginning of Jesus' public ministry is marked off by an elaborate dating to emphasise its significance. It is inaugurated by John's preaching that puts emphasis on social concerns. After his baptism during prayer, the Spirit descends in bodily form and the Father's voice affirms his divine sonship. Luke traces his genealogy back to Adam and God. The temptation scene corrects a false understanding of Jesus' identity and mission. Jesus refuses to use his status for personal gain thereby demonstrating that he is the obedient Son.

He returns to Galilee where most of his ministry will take place until he departs for Jerusalem. Filled with the Spirit, he begins his mission in the synagogue at Nazareth with a programmatic sermon reflecting the Jubilee year amnesty for the oppressed, but this only provokes hostility in the audience. Jesus goes on to Capernaum where his preaching and healings mark him out as teacher and healer. After the call of the first disciples and the cleansing of a leper, Luke presents a series of five controversies with the Pharisees. They involve a paralytic, the call of Levi, fasting, picking grain and healing on the sabbath. Next he recounts the choice of the Twelve and healings before preaching to the crowd on the plain which is directed to the disciples. Four beatitudes and accompanying woes sound a note of good news for the poor and judgement against the rich. These are followed by general ethical precepts: loving enemies, not judging others, bearing fruit and the necessity of doing.

Luke continues with a selection of miracle stories and parables that illustrate Jesus' power and help to reveal his identity. The centurion's servant and the raising of the widow's son elicits the acknowledgement that a great prophet has risen among the people, as well as showing Jesus' compassionate care. The relationship of John to Jesus is clarified and Jesus praises John. There is the story of the sinful woman who is forgiven and there is the record that some Galilean women follow Jesus. Another series of parables and miracles follows: the parable of the sower and explanation, the parable of the lamp, Jesus' family, storm at sea, Gerasene demoniac, Jairus' daughter and the woman with the haemorrhage. All these show the grandeur of Jesus as he exercises power over the sea, demons, sickness and death. He now imparts some of his power when he sends out the Twelve on a mission.

In the meantime, we are informed of Herod's perplexity. The feeding of the five thousand follows with Peter's confession of Jesus as the Messiah of God, the first prediction of the passion and the necessity of the cross. The transfiguration scene, set in the context of Jesus praying, gives us a glimpse of the glory present in Jesus' earthly career as he converses with Moses and Elijah about his 'exodus' in Jerusalem. God's voice identifies him as Son and chosen One. The cure of the boy with the demon reflects 'the majesty of God'. After the second prediction, there is a dispute about greatness among the disciples, but Jesus assures them that the least among them is truly great, and even an outside exorcist who uses Jesus' name has a place as well.

Jesus now sets his face towards Jerusalem as one who knows and accepts his destiny. This journey is a Lukan construct, an expansion of the Markan journey that allows him to insert large blocks of teaching material peculiar to him. It is a time of preparation for the disciples. There is a hostile encounter in a Samaritan village followed by a dialogue with three who would have followed Jesus, but were unable to meet his absolute demands. The size of the harvest is the reason for a further mission of seventy two disciples, and this is followed by woes against unrepentant cities. On their return, Jesus thanks the Father for the revelation granted to disciples. A lawyer's question about eternal life evokes Jesus' response about love of God and neighbour that leads into the parable of the good Samaritan. The story of Martha and Mary shows the importance of heeding the word of Jesus. Teaching on prayer including the Lucan 'Our Father' follows, and the promise of the Holy Spirit to those who ask it. A controversy passage and sayings about the evil spirit ends with a beatitude from a woman in the crowd. Jesus issues warnings for his generation and woes against the Pharisees ending with a caution to beware of their hypocrisy. There is an exhortation to courage in the face of persecution and the unforgivable blasphemy against the Holy Spirit. The parable of the rich fool makes the point that attachment to material things is incompatible with living for God, as does being overanxious about life.

Luke continues this section with a warning on the necessity of faithful watchfulness. Jesus' ministry can also be a source of division. It is crucial to be able to read the signs of the times, to settle matters with an opponent. He then gives examples to promote repentance and the parable of the fig tree offers one more chance to bear fruit. Jesus teaches on the sabbath and heals a crippled woman which provokes the synagogue ruler's indignation. The two parables of the mustard seed and the leaven give assurance of the spread and ultimate greatness of the kingdom despite small beginnings.

The second section of the journey narrative introduces material on exclusion and entry into the kingdom. Herod's desire to kill Jesus prompts a lament over Jerusalem because of its treatment of the prophets. This is followed by the sabbath cure of a man with dropsy, instructions about conduct at dinner, the parable of the great banquet and sayings about the cost of discipleship. Three parables – lost sheep, lost coin, and lost son – are addressed to the Pharisees and scribes who object to Jesus keeping company with sinners. They give a lesson on God's loving mercy. The dishonest steward is praised for his prudent initiative and this is followed by diverse sayings on wealth, Law and divorce. The parable of the rich man and Lazarus illustrates the damning effects of wealth that leads to indifference towards the poor. Jesus speaks of scandal, forgiveness, faith and duty.

The third section begins with the cleansing of ten lepers and the Samaritan who alone shows gratitude. There are warnings against being deceived, bogus claims and thoughtless living. The parable of the persistent widow encourages perseverance in prayer, while that of the Pharisee and publican exemplifies God's mercy and generosity, and children offer an example of dependence on God. This leads to the ruler's question on what is necessary for eternal life and the obstacle presented by love of riches. What Jesus is to sacrifice is enunciated in the third prediction of the passion. As he enters Jericho, Jesus heals a blind man and encounters Zacchaeus who provides an example of the correct use of wealth, as does the parable of the coins. The disciples are challenged to make profitable use of all Jesus has revealed to them.

There is a royal entry into Jerusalem, but Jesus predicts the destruction of the city and cleanses the Temple. His teaching there provokes questions on authority on the part of the chief priests and scribes only to be counterchallenged by Jesus about John the Baptist. The parable of the tenants is a thinly-veiled criticism of these authorities who now try to trap Jesus with questions about taxes and resurrection. Jesus in turn questions them about David's son. These confrontations come to an end with the condemnation of the scribes' love of ostentatiousness contrasted with the widow who gave all she had. The prediction of the destruction of the Temple leads to a discourse on the last things, persecution, tribulation, the coming of the Son of Man, and ends with an exhortation to be vigilant.

In his passion account, Luke combines the Markan source with special traditions. There is a conspiracy against Jesus as preparations are made for the Last Supper. Stress is placed on the soteriological aspect of Jesus' death and on the eucharist which commemorates it. Jesus praises his disciples' fidelity and promises them a place at his table in the kingdom. He foretells Peter's denial and instructs the disciples on the coming crisis.

There is the prayer and arrest at the Mount of Olives, followed by the Jewish and Roman trials. Jesus is present when Peter denies him. A set of charges are presented to Pilate who on three occasions finds no case against Jesus. Pilate sends Jesus to Herod who questions and mocks him. Finally, Pilate hands Jesus over to the Jews to be crucified. On the cross Jesus forgives his executioners, and promises paradise to the repentant thief, before entrusting himself into his Father's hands. He is then buried by Joseph.

Luke concentrates the appearances of the risen Jesus in Jerusalem. The women at the empty tomb do not remain silent but tell the apostles. Jesus appears to two disciples on the road to Emmaus. He appeals to the scriptures to explain what has happened and they recognise him in the breaking of bread. Jesus appears to the assembled disciples on Easter Sunday evening. Luke insists on the reality of the risen Jesus who explains the scriptures to them to prepare them to be his witnesses. The gospel ends with the ascension on the Mount of Olives. Jesus blesses the disciples and is carried up to heaven while the disciples return to Jerusalem. The gospel, which had its beginning in the Temple, also ends there with the disciples praising God.

JESUS IN LUKE'S GOSPEL

The Narrative as a Whole

Although Luke generally follows the basic Markan outline, he omits some episodes, introduces many new ones and arranges them in a different manner. Consequently, the story he tells is a new narrative with its own distinctive christological portrait. As well, by adding the story of the church in Acts, Luke relates what Mark and Matthew never describe in detail, that is, the time after Jesus' resurrection. In this way, Luke extends the story of Jesus by recounting the vital role the risen Lord plays in the life of the early church. While the gospel clearly focuses on Jesus during his ministry, Acts recounts the church's witness to its risen Lord. Both narratives have their own distinct story to tell, yet the person of Jesus spans both. The risen Lord to whom the church bears witness cannot be separated from the earthly Jesus who called the community into being in the first place. The Lukan christology is therefore embedded in both these narratives.

In the gospel the announcement of salvation occurs in the heart of Israel, the Jerusalem Temple. This salvation is the fulfilment of promises made to Abraham (1:55), takes place within the house of David (1:69) and is good news for those awaiting redemption (2:38). The birth of Jesus, the Davidic Messiah, fulfils God's promises to Israel and the first to hear of the coming salvation are pious Israelites who have faithfully observed the Law (1:6). The angel announces the birth of the Messiah to the virgin Mary (1:26-38). She will conceive a Son who will be named Jesus. He will be called Son of the Most High, the Lord will give him the throne of David his father to rule over the house of Jacob forever. This is in fulfilment of the promises made by the prophet Nathan to David (cf 2 Sam 7:12-16). When Mary inquires how this will come about, the angel informs her that the Holy Spirit will come upon her and the power of the Most High will overshadow her. Thus the child will be called God's Son. The Davidic king will also be God's Son whose kingdom will have no end. How this comes about is not immediately clear. After this, Elizabeth greets Mary as 'the mother of my Lord' (1:43).

The first part of the infancy narratives indicates that the birth of the Messiah and his predecessor are a continuation of God's faithfulness to Israel – Jesus is the Davidic Messiah who will fulfil God's promises to Israel. Zechariah proclaims that Jesus will bring Israel salvation from its enemies so that it can worship God in holiness and righteousness (1:74-75). The birth of the Messiah takes place in the Davidic city of Bethlehem. The first to hear of it are the shepherds to whom the angel announces the joyful news that a Saviour has been born who is Messiah and Lord (2:11). Since Jesus is Jewish, he is circumcised and presented to the Lord in accordance with the Law (2:21-24). The aged

Simeon recognises that Jesus is the Lord's Messiah, a light of revelation for the gentiles and glory for his people (2:32), and Anna is aware of the redemptive role he is to play. The twelve-year-old Jesus is found by his parents in his Father's house. In the infancy narrative, then, Jesus is portrayed as the Lord's Messiah, the royal descendant of David, Saviour and Redeemer of his people. But this Messiah is also God's Son who will save gentiles as well as Jews.

The Spirit descends on Jesus at his baptism while he is at prayer and the Father declares Jesus to be his beloved Son. Jesus is the Spirit-filled Messiah, the Son of God in whom the Father is well pleased. Luke provides Jesus with a genealogy that goes back to David and Abraham and even further to Adam and God. Jesus is God's Son (3:38). The emphasis on the divine sonship continues in the testing in the wilderness (4:3,9), and Jesus proves who he is by his obedience.

Empowered by the Spirit he teaches in the synagogue of Nazareth where he proclaims that the prophetic text of Is 60:1-2 finds fulfilment in his messianic ministry of preaching good news to the poor, healing the broken-hearted and announcing the jubilee year (4:16-21). Nevertheless, he is rejected by the townspeople and this establishes a pattern for his ministry. Yet despite his rejection at Nazareth, Jesus continues his ministry in Galilee (4:31-9:50). He expels demons, cures the sick, proclaims the kingdom, calls disciples, cleanses lepers, forgives sins, chooses twelve disciples, preaches the sermon on the plain and raises the dead.

Notwithstanding his good work, the response to Jesus is mixed. Some recognise the power of Jesus' word and glorify God. They acknowledge a great prophet in their midst, and exclaim that God has visited his people (7:16). But the scribes and Pharisees question his right to forgive sins, his eating with tax collectors and sinners and his behaviour on the sabbath. Clearly, they have not understood the nature of his ministry. As the Galilean ministry closes, the question of Jesus' identity surfaces: Is he John risen from the dead, or perhaps one of the prophets?

Peter confesses him as 'the Messiah of God' (9:20), and Jesus teaches his disciples that he must suffer, die and rise again. At the transfiguration scene, Jesus discusses with Moses and Elijah his forthcoming 'exodus' in Jerusalem (9:31), while the Father declares that Jesus is his beloved Son. By the end of his Galilean ministry, there is little doubt about Jesus' identity – he is the Spirit-filled Messiah, a prophetic Messiah and the Son of God.

The journey to Jerusalem begins in a decisive manner as Jesus sets his face towards it (9:51). This seems to indicate a profound consciousness on the part of Jesus of his messianic destiny to suffer, die, rise, and be taken up into heaven where he will be enthroned as Lord and Messiah. Throughout the journey Jesus instructs his disciples to leave their homes, family and possessions, to proclaim the kingdom, and he warns the crowds of the consequences of their failure to repent. The journey narrative presents Jesus as the prophetic Messiah and preacher of the kingdom summoning Israel to repentance, but also as a compassionate Messiah who brings salvation to those in need. The journey ends with a prophetic lament that foretells the city's destruction because it did not recognise its messianic visitation. After cleansing the Temple, Jesus teaches the people there, but his ministry only meets with hostility from the religious leaders who attempt to discredit him, and challenge his authority by posing questions. Jesus manifests his superior knowledge and the leaders fall silent. He challenges them to explain how they can claim that the Messiah is David's son since David calls him Lord (20:41-44). The implication of the unanswered question is that the Messiah is not only David's son, but also Son of God. Jesus ends with a prophetic discourse on the Temple's destruction and the coming of the Son of Man (21:5-36). When the times of the gentiles are fulfilled, there will be cosmic signs heralding the coming of the Son of Man, and his followers will know that their redemption is at hand.

The Messiah who resolutely set his face towards Jerusalem is arrested, led to Pilate and accused of misleading Israel in opposing taxes to Caesar and claiming to be the Messiah, a king (23:2).

Although Pilate is not convinced of his guilt, he hands him over to be crucified as King of the Jews. The manner in which he suffers and dies leads a criminal to acknowledge Jesus' innocence (23:41), a Roman soldier confesses Jesus to be truly righteous (23:47), and the crowds return home beating their breasts. At the empty tomb the angels remind the women that the Son of Man had to be handed over to sinners to be crucified and rise on the third day (24:7). On the road to Emmaus, the risen Jesus instructs two disciples that he had to suffer so as to enter into his glory. To the eleven disciples he explains that Moses, the prophets and the psalms had already written of the Messiah's suffering and resurrection, and that repentance and forgiveness should be preached in his name to all the nations (24:44-47). At the end of the gospel Jesus is taken up to heaven, thereby attaining the ultimate purpose of his journey to Jerusalem.

It seems, then, despite Israel's rejection of its Messiah and the apparent failure of his ministry to bring them to repentance, that everything happened in accordance with the divine plan already outlined in the Old Testament. Suffering and death were a necessary prelude to the glory that Acts describes as a royal enthronement at God's right hand (Acts 2:34-36). The result of Jesus' actions is the forgiveness of sins and the bestowal of salvation. Jesus the Messiah redeems Israel from the rule of Satan and the burden of sin in order to lead them to God.

The Acts of the Apostles completes the gospel portrait of Jesus. The angel's prediction (Lk 1:32-33) that God will give Jesus David's throne and that he will reign forever, is fulfilled in the exaltation to God's right hand and messianic enthronement. In his Pentecost sermon, Peter sees the death of the Messiah as being in conformity with God's plan (Acts 2:14-36). Furthermore, God's raising Jesus from the dead is in accordance with Psalm 16. Raised from the dead, Jesus is exalted to God's right hand as David prophesied in Psalm 110:1, and Peter concludes: 'Therefore, let all Israel know with certainty that God has made him both Lord and Messiah, this Jesus whom you crucified' (Acts 2:36). Jesus is not only Messiah, but Lord as well so that the

words of the prophet Joel, once spoken of God, are now applied
to Jesus (cf Acts 2:21). Moreover, the exalted Jesus will come
again to restore all things (cf Acts 3:19-26). The prophet of whom
Moses spoke is Jesus, the Messiah, the eschatological prophet, a
leader like Moses, leading from death to life. Thus in the early
speeches in Acts Jesus is the one who fulfils the prophets. Seated
at God's right hand, he sends the Spirit to continue his work
through authorised witnesses. Although it should be noted that
Acts is no longer the story of Jesus, it is the story of the church
which completes and explains it.

Titles of Jesus

Luke adopts titles for Jesus from the tradition and the christological confessions of the early church and incorporates them
into his christology. Jesus is the promised Messiah of Israel offering salvation from God and so the God of Israel is faithful to
his promises that have now become a reality in the person of
Jesus. Jesus is God's Messiah and so is properly called Son of
God because he was born through the power of the Spirit, and
this is confirmed at the baptism and transfiguration scenes. This
messianic Son of God is Saviour of his people. Anointed with the
Spirit, he brings good news to the poor, frees people from
Satan's bondage, cures the sick and suffers upon the cross. The
fullness of salvation will occur when Jesus returns at the end of
the ages. Israel's Messiah is a prophetic figure who calls Israel to
repentance only to meet with opposition and rejection. But unlike past prophetic figures, he is the Son of God and those who
repudiate his message are rejecting the eschatological agent sent
by God to his people. In Acts, the Messiah is Lord because he is
enthroned at God's right hand. But Luke introduces the title
Lord into his gospel as well (cf Lk 1:43, 10:1), thereby pointing to
the unity of the earthly Jesus with the risen Christ. Jesus is already Messiah and Lord at his birth (cf Lk 2:11). Since the resurrection is the moment when God enthrones his Son, Israel
should now know who Jesus always was. Yet we should not

overlook the fact that Jesus is also portrayed as a very human figure in Luke's gospel.[16]

Messiah. Although not the most frequently used title for Jesus, it is, nonetheless, an important title for Luke: 'Was it not necessary that the Messiah should suffer these things and then enter into his glory?'(Lk 24:26). Of all the evangelists, Luke alone tells us that the disciples were called Christians, or followers of the Messiah (cf Acts 11:26). The title Messiah is derived from Palestinian Judaism and was used in the Old Testament for anointed agents of God. In the pre-Christian centuries there emerged a messianic expectation, a future David sent by God for the restoration of Israel and the triumph of God's reign. This idea developed out of the Davidic tradition (cf 2 Sam 7; royal psalms, messianic prophecies). By Jesus' time it would have denoted an expected anointed agent of God in the kingly tradition to restore Israel. Luke already found it in the tradition. Jesus is addressed by Peter as 'the Messiah of God' (Lk 9:20), but Jesus corrects it by announcing his destiny as Son of Man to avoid possible political overtones. In the Lukan trial scene, the Jewish leaders accuse him 'saying that he himself is the Messiah, a king' (Lk 23:2). Luke places Jesus' kingship which comes from God side by side with political kingship of which he is accused before Pilate and subsequently condemned to death (cf Lk 23:38). Jesus' answer to the High Priest's question is evasive for the same reason: 'If I tell you, you will not believe, and if I question you, you will not answer' (22:67).

Luke took the conception of a suffering Messiah from the early preaching in spite of the fact that no precedent for it existed in Judaism at the time. After his death, Christ became the title *par excellence* for Jesus and even his name. Crucified as a king, he quickly became for his followers 'the Messiah'. This perception was coloured by the resurrection faith. It became part of the Christian preaching soon after (cf 1 Cor 15:3). The title is expressly linked to Jesus' resurrection in Acts 2:31, 36. Having composed

16. Cf J. A. Fitzmyer, *The Gospel according to Luke, 1-9,* New York: Doubleday, 1981, pp 192-258

the infancy narratives with hindsight, Luke has the angels declare to the shepherds: 'For you is born this day in the city of David a Saviour who is Christ, the Lord' (Lk.2:11). For Luke, the title Messiah designates Jesus as God's anointed agent sent to announce salvation in the context of preaching God's kingdom. It is, then, the Christian Messiah that Luke proclaims, the one who suffered and died but raised from the dead and exalted to God's right hand. God makes him 'both Lord and Messiah, this Jesus whom you crucified' (Acts 2:36). It is the same Messiah who will come again at the end of time: 'that he may send you the Messiah appointed for you, that is, Jesus, who must remain in heaven until the time of universal restoration that God announced' (Acts 3:20-21).

Closely related to Messiah are the titles Son of David and King which Luke also borrowed from the tradition. Both are implied in the angelic message about receiving the throne of David, his father (cf Lk 1:32). His birth takes place in Bethlehem, David's city (Lk 2:4). In Luke 19:38 Jesus enters Jerusalem as king, bringing peace to a city that does not recognise the time of its visitation. The title king is also associated with the parables of the kingdom, and the penitent thief asks Jesus to remember him when he comes into his kingdom (Lk 23:42).

Son of God. Jesus is Son of God already in the proclamation to Mary: 'He will be great and will be called Son of the Most High ... the child to be born will be holy, he will be called the Son of God' (1:32, 35). This title appears at Jesus' baptism, the temptation scene, in the recognition by demons, the transfiguration scene, the cry of jubilation, and in the procedure before the Sanhedrin. At the resurrection, the divine sonship of Jesus is revealed in all its saving power. For Luke there is no contradiction in saying that Jesus was Son of God from the moment of his conception and his being designated Son of God at the resurrection (cf Acts 13:33). Jesus also refers to himself as the Son (Lk 10:22).

The title 'Son of God' had a long pre-history in the ancient Near East and in the Old Testament. It was claimed for pharaohs, kings and mythical figures. In Israel it was applied to

the people, its king and pious individuals, but it was never predicated of the expected Messiah. Applied to Jesus in the early
preaching, it was adopted by Luke in Acts where he relates it to
the resurrection by applying Psalm 2:7 to Jesus (cf Acts 13:33).
He has also made it part of his early christology beginning with
the angelic message to Mary (Lk 1:32, 35). In the gospel the title
attributes to Jesus a unique relationship with God (cf Lk 10:22).
That Jesus is not the Son of God in the way the Davidic kings
were regarded, that is, as adopted sons of God, is evident in
Luke's explicit relating of the title to the conception of Jesus.

Saviour. This is a distinctive title of Luke, although used only
at the time of Jesus' birth by the angels: 'For to you is born this
day in the city of David, a Saviour' (Lk 2:11), and in Acts 5:31,
13:23. It was frequently applied in the Greco-Roman world to
gods, kings, philosophers, and others. In the Old Testament God
is the Saviour of his people (cf Is 45:15), but 'saviour' is also
associated with Joshua and the judges whom God raised up to
deliver his people in times of distress. The Christian usage may
have been influenced by both. According to Luke, Jesus is the
true Saviour who surpasses the emperor, but he adds 'Christ,
the Lord' to protect Jesus from being accommodated to the emperor cult of the time. From David's descendants God has raised
up a Saviour for Israel, as he promised. During his ministry
Jesus acts as Saviour when he delivers people from all kinds of
evil and sickness. Positively, the salvation he brings is a restoration to wholeness and wellbeing, especially to a restored relationship with God which implies deliverance from sin as well:
'God exalted him at his right hand as Leader and Saviour, that
he might give repentance to Israel and the forgiveness of sins'
(Acts 5:31).

For Luke, therefore, Jesus is the one who brings to fulfilment
the promises of salvation. In and through Jesus, the Saviour, the
mercy and saving power of God is present: the blind see, the
lame walk, lepers are cleansed, the deaf hear, the dead are
raised, and the gospel is proclaimed to the poor (cf 7:22). Above
all the goodness of God is revealed in his mercy (6:36) pro-

claimed by Jesus and expressed unforgettably in the parable of the merciful Father (15:11-32). God is revealed as a kind, all for-giving Father who welcomes home his wayward son and res-tores him to the full dignity of sonship. The parables of the lost sheep and lost coin (15:4-10) show God's great joy over recover-ing what was lost. The bringing of grace, 'the year of the Lord's favour' (4:19) and the accompanying joy is the task of the Saviour sent by God.

Prophet. Luke places notable emphasis on Jesus as the prophet-like-Moses whom God will raise up (cf Acts 3:22-23, 7:37 which explicitly cites Deut 18:15-18). In the gospel, Jesus is depicted as using the title for himself, at least by implication, when he compares himself with Elijah and Elisha in the Nazareth scene (4:24-27). The story has been transposed and ex-panded by Luke into a programmatic statement on the nature of his ministry (4:16-30). Filled with the Spirit, Jesus reads from Isaiah 61:1-2 and announces that this prophecy is fulfilled in him 'today'. After the raising of the widow's son in Nain, the crowd exclaims: 'A great prophet has arisen among us' (7:16). Some people regard him as Elijah returned to life, while others think he is one of the prophets of old (cf Lk 9:8, 19), and he is certainly a prophet mighty in word and deed (Lk 24:19). Luke also has Jesus refer to himself as a prophet and links it to his destiny: 'I must be on my way ... because it is impossible for a prophet to be killed outside of Jerusalem' (Lk 13:33). At the end of his jour-ney, Jesus voices a prophetic lament over the city which does not recognise the time of its visitation (Lk 19:41-44). While Jesus is in custody his captors mock him: 'Prophesy! Who is it that struck you?' (Lk 22:64). That Luke casts Jesus in the role of a prophet-like-Moses is implied from the transfiguration scene when Jesus converses with Moses and Elijah about his upcoming 'exodus' like Moses', and the heavenly voice commands: 'Listen to him' (Lk 9:31, 35, cf Deut 18:15).

Luke then understands Jesus as the prophet anointed with the Spirit. His mission is to proclaim deliverance to the outcasts and afflicted which in turn causes division among the people.

The prophetic pattern is continued as Jesus proclaims blessings to the poor and woes to the rich (Lk 6:20, 24). Just as Elisha healed a foreigner through the intercession of a Jewish girl (cf 2 Kgs 5:1-14), Jesus heals a gentile centurion's servant because of Jewish mediation (Lk 7:1-10). As Elijah raised a widow's son (cf 1 Kgs 17:17-24), Jesus raises the widow's son at Nain (Lk 7:11-17). The conflict generated by his prophetic ministry is illustrated when Jesus is accepted by the sinful woman, while the Pharisee host does not recognise Jesus as a prophet sent by God (Lk 7:36-50). As Jesus journeys to Jerusalem to face rejection at the hands of the authorities, Luke has Jesus the prophet gathering the true people of God around him. After his death, Jesus is vindicated as God's prophet in the resurrection, he is 'the prophet whom God raised up' in power (Acts 3:22-23). The risen Christ demonstrates 'from Moses and the prophets' how his sufferings fulfilled the scriptures (Lk 24:25-26, 44). In Acts Jesus' prophetic role takes a new form through the power of the Spirit at work in the apostles.

The image of Jesus as Prophet allows Luke to focus on the social dimension of Jesus' message, which is a reversal of human values. Luke has preserved sayings of Jesus about the rich and poor that go back to the time of Jesus. Jesus' efforts on behalf of the poor, though, did not make him into a social reformer. His prophetic call was directed at the rich to share their wealth by giving alms (cf 11:41, 12:33), to sell all their possessions and to distribute their money to the poor (14:33, 18:22). The renunciation of possessions becomes a requirement for those who would follow Jesus as the beatitude of the poor and the woes against the rich illustrate (6:20, 24). The term 'poor' in Luke connotes actual poverty, the really destitute, as well as the sick and suffering who could not provide for themselves but were dependent on the generosity of others.

Luke has written extensively on wealth. He adds to the synoptic tradition special material: woes against the rich (6:24), the rich fool (12:16-21), dinner hospitality (14:12-14), the rich man and Lazarus (16:19-31), Zacchaeus (19:1-10). The rich are those who enjoy material well-being, but Luke is more concerned with the attitude produced by affluence which leads to greed (12:15), preoccupation with worldly cares and enjoyment of life (8:14, 12:19, 16:19, 21:34). The danger with an opulent lifestyle (12:19) is that one neglects of the poor (16:20-21), has desire for honours (14:7-8), becomes arrogant (cf 14:16-20) and consequently forgets about God. This is fundamentally the rejection of Jesus' call (cf 18:22-23) and means that one cannot enter into the kingdom of God (18:25). Luke advocates both giving to the poor and the proper administration of property (cf 16:9-13). This latter view is confirmed in Acts.

By casting him in the prophetic mould, Luke also sees Jesus as the spokesperson for God who can speak God's word with authority. In the centuries preceding the Christian era, there arose the expectation of an eschatological prophet (cf 1 Macc 14:41; Qumran). Jesus is the bringer of God's definitive word to humankind, thereby launching a new phase of salvation history.

Lord. Luke frequently uses Lord in Luke-Acts to designate both God and Jesus, thus putting Jesus on a par with God, but never identifies him with the Father. He applies it to Jesus after the resurrection (Acts 2:36) and often retrojects it into Jesus' ministry. Many people address Jesus as Lord in the gospel and historically this would have been little more than a title of respect. Now with hindsight it can be read in a religious sense as Lord which speaks of Jesus' transcendent character, especially his risen status. By placing it back in the time of Jesus' ministry, Luke surrounds Jesus with an aura that already foreshadows his risen existence. It is used to designate the newborn child: 'For you is born this day in the city of David a Saviour, who is the Messiah, the Lord' (2:11; cf 1:43). For Luke, the actual transformation takes place at Jesus' ascension (Lk 24:51; Acts 1:9-11) when he returns to take his place at God's right hand.

The Lord to Come. Jesus will return again at the parousia (cf Acts1:11). In the eschatological discourse, the Son of Man will come with power and great glory (21:27) when the time of the gentiles is fulfilled (21:24), and signs will appear in the cosmos

(21:25-27). In all of this Luke generally follows Mark, but adds: 'Now when these things begin to take place, stand up and raise your heads, because your redemption is drawing near' (21:28). In Luke the parousia acquires a salvific significance. Believers will then experience the fullness of salvation already begun here below. The exalted Lord will return at the end of the age to complete his work of salvation, which Luke calls 'times of refreshing' (Acts 3:20). The parables of the parousia (12:15-48) emphasise the readiness that the coming of the Lord demands.

In the parables of the rich fool (12:16-21) and the dishonest manager (16:1-8), the focus is on the death of the individual when God will demand an account. This perspective is also present in the parable of the rich man and Lazarus (16:19-31), and the promise of paradise to the good thief 'today' (23:42-43). Thus, in part at least, Luke has shifted the focus of the parousia to the time of death. As well as cosmic-universal eschatology, there is also individual eschatology with the onset of death. Each person experiences the end of time at death, and so this becomes an added incentive to consider the transitoriness of life especially with regard to earthly goods. Nevertheless, everyone is inserted into the course of history that will also come to an end. The coming of the Lord at the parousia provides the background and the standard for the death of every single person.

Jesus' proclamation of the kingdom, therefore, is comprised of a present and future aspect when the kingdom will reach its perfection. It is essentially an eschatological message that Jesus preached and so the parousia was eagerly awaited and expected in the early church. Cosmic events will herald its beginning (21:25-27). But for Luke at any rate, these will take place in the indefinite future and only deceivers say 'the time is near' (21:8). Wars and insurrections are not signs of the end: 'These must take place first, but the end will not follow immediately' (21:9). Before the parousia arrives 'the times of the gentiles must be fulfilled' (21:24). Thus the actual time of the parousia is left open (cf 19:11-27). The parables in chapter twelve contain the possibility of delay and a moment of crisis. Nevertheless, one should always be ready for the coming of the Lord. Delay could cause a slackening of one's attention. The turning from the cosmic to the individual may have been occasioned by a realisation on the part of the church of the delay of the parousia. The church and its mission are oriented to the parousia when Jesus as Lord of the church will one day return (cf Acts 3:19-21). In the meantime, the age of the church with its missionary outreach will advance the work of salvation begun by Jesus during his ministry.

Human Traits. Luke presents Jesus as a Palestinian Jew born in Bethlehem of David's stock and raised at Nazareth. He speaks of Jesus as 'a man attested to you by God with deeds of power, wonders, and signs that God did through him among you, as you yourselves know' (Acts 2:22). He portrays Jesus as a human being concerned for others during his ministry to the extent of offering his life on the cross in a spirit of supreme human dedication. Jesus is someone who shows qualities of mercy, love, charm and joy in dealing with others. This is evident in the memorable parables of Jesus preserved by Luke: the parable of the two debtors (7:41-43), the good Samaritan (10:29-37), the barren fig tree (13:6-9), the parables of the lost sheep, lost coin, lost son and merciful Father (15:4-32), the Pharisee and the tax collector (18:9-14). The story of Zacchaeus (19:1-10) and the two disciples on the road to Emmaus (24:13-35) show the delicacy of Jesus, the exemplar of virtue for imitation by Christians.

Jesus' humanity and graciousness is also seen in his attitude to women. In no other gospel are women so prominent and play such a considerable role. As Jesus travelled from village to village with the Twelve, some women also accompany him to serve him and his disciples (8:1-3). Women accompany Jesus to the cross (23:49) and are the first to experience the risen Christ (24:1-6). Through this accompaniment of Jesus during his earthly career and their witnessing of his death and burial, women take their place alongside Jesus' disciples. They become a key link in the transmission of the resurrection message to the disciples (24:9). They are present with the apostles as they await the descent of the Spirit (Acts 1:14) and are fully integrated into the growing church. Luke develops a picture of Jesus and women that is totally new.

Already in the infancy narrative, we encounter Mary, the mother of Jesus, and Elizabeth who calls Mary blessed (1:42). Mary is the favoured one who has conceived a child through the Holy Spirit and is greeted by Elizabeth as the mother of the Lord. Mary treasures all the happenings in her heart (2:19, 51). Luke's lofty portrayal of Mary distinguishes her from all other women in the gospel. During his public life, Mary is in the background, although she is included in the spiritual family of those who hear the word of God and keep it (8:19-21). She is also praised for her motherhood by a woman in the crowd (11:27-28).

Luke's special material includes the widow of Zerepath, the widow of Nain, the sinful woman in the house of Simon the Pharisee, the women who accompany Jesus, the story of Martha and Mary, the woman in the crowd, the crippled woman, the story of the lost coin, the persistent widow and the women on the way to the crucifixion. The graceful visitation of God in the case of the grieving mother and widow to whom Jesus restores her only son, shows Jesus' devotion to women (7:16). Jesus' compassion is also evident when he is anointed by the sinful woman who is socially ostracised (7:36-50). Jesus accepts her as a human being and forgives her sins. The visit of Jesus to the house of Martha and Mary elicits praise for Mary who listens to Jesus' words. Luke includes this pericope (10:38-42) because he appreciates the sensitivity of women's listening skills and places it above a readiness to serve. The account of the persistent widow in the parable (18:1-5) is another illustration of a woman who through Jesus finds God's mercy.

The dignity of women is also recognised by Jesus in the healing stories. The woman with the haemorrhage is addressed as 'daughter' (8:48), the crippled woman is called 'a daughter of Abraham' (13:16) which is surprising given the significance of male descendants in that culture. She belongs to the people of God every bit as much as Zacchaeus whom Jesus calls 'a son of Abraham' (19:9). In Jesus' encounter with women, their human qualities become evident in their support of the disciples, their spiritual participation in Jesus' destiny and their presence at his burial. Women are often paired with men in Luke. Evidently he wishes to portray them as being equal to men. Women are called to discipleship. Such close contact with women was unusual given the social conditions of the time. Although they do not publicly proclaim the kingdom as the disciples did, they are still present with Jesus and support him in his mission. Thus Jesus breaks through the social barriers of contemporary Jewish society.

Luke devotes considerable attention to Jesus at prayer, to the extent that it becomes a special feature in his portrait of Jesus. Jesus prays at all important occasions, in crucial situations and turning points in his ministry. He is introduced as the one who prays at his baptism (3:21), in a deserted place (5:16), before choosing the apostles (6:12), before Peter's confession (9:18), at the transfiguration (9:28-29), before the Lord's Prayer (11:1), he prays for Peter (22:32), and on the cross (23:34, 46). In close contact with the Father, Jesus begins his mission and continues this practice up to the Mount of Olives (22:42), until finally he confidently on the cross entrusts his spirit into his Father's hands (23:46).

Jesus also leads his church in prayer. The disciples want to learn how to pray themselves when they observe Jesus at prayer (11:1). Jesus teaches them the Lord's Prayer and the promise of the Holy Spirit is given at the end (11:13). The prayerful Jesus becomes a model for the disciples. Stephen dies like Jesus forgiving his executioners (Acts 7:60). Jesus' prayer on the Mount of Olives is framed by an admonition to the disciples: 'Pray that you may not come into the time of trial' (22:40, 46). The prayer of Jesus enclosed by this admonition demonstrates the kind of prayer that allows temptation to be overcome. God will grant justice to those 'who cry to him day and night' (18:7-8), the disciples are to pray always and not lose heart (cf 18:1), for persistent prayer will always be heard. Jesus teaches them how to pray and what they are to pray for (11:1-13). Believers are to be alert at all times and pray that they will have the strength to persevere (cf 21:36). They are to pray especially for the gift of the Spirit (11:13). Luke wants to establish a pattern of prayer in all situations. Prayer and praying are mentioned frequently in Acts, so that the impression is given of a praying community in imitation of its Founder.

Luke's portrait of Jesus is then enriched with special features. He appropriates traditions from Mark and Q and shapes them, together with his special traditions, to paint his own distinctive portrait of Jesus. This is especially noticeable in the portrayal of Jesus as Messiah, Son of God, Saviour, Prophet and Lord and in his emphasis on the humanity of Jesus in his relationships and in prayer. Luke's human picture of Jesus makes him an attractive person for imitation by Christians. This has led scholars to regard Luke as less a historian and more of a biographer. They argue that his work fits within the category of ancient biography (*bioi*), in particular, those written within the philosophical schools to honour their founder which included as well an interpretation of his teachings offered to pupils for imitation.

CHAPTER FIVE

The Gospel of John

INTRODUCTION

The gospel of John is very different in character from the synoptics. It is more of a deep theological reflection on the life and ministry of Jesus that developed, over a long period of time, in community circles different from those that produced the synoptics. Like them, it has its roots in what Jesus said and did. However, these have undergone selection and refinement until the tradition was shaped into a written gospel that now stands as an independent witness to Jesus.

John differs from the synoptics in style and content. Jesus speaks more solemnly and is conscious of pre-existing with God before coming into the world. His public ministry alternates between Galilee and Judea with the major portion in Judea, thus differing from the synoptics' extensive ministry in Galilee. The cleansing of the Temple is placed at the beginning of the ministry that in turn is connected with the great Jewish pilgrimage feasts – Passover, Tabernacles, Dedication – and spans a three year period. The Last Supper is not a paschal meal, and Jesus' death coincides with the slaughter of the Passover lambs in the Temple. A more significant difference is evident in Jesus' deeds and words. John has no exorcisms. The miracle stories are called 'signs' and they point to the identity and mission of Jesus. Some of the miracle stories are unique to John: Cana, the man born blind, and Lazarus. Jesus' words are developed into lengthy discourses rather than the parables and sayings we find in the synoptics.

Behind the gospel stands the figure of the Beloved Disciple. His appreciation of Jesus stands at the beginning of the Johannine tradition. Since the end of the second century, the Beloved Disciple has been associated with John, the son of

Zebedee, one of the Twelve.[17] The gospel, however, does not identify the Beloved Disciple, who is the source of the tradition, with John the apostle. From the gospel itself the Beloved Disciple is at least an eyewitness of the end of Jesus' ministry. He is first mentioned at the Last Supper (13:23). He is familiar with Palestinian geography and Jewish feasts and ceremonies, theology and customs. He knows the High Priest's family (18:15), is present at the cross (19:35), goes with Peter to the empty tomb (20:3), and is present in Galilee when Jesus appears (21:7). He is called the Beloved Disciple by the circle that honoured him as the bearer and interpreter of the message of Jesus. He is not the author of the gospel in its present form. The gospel is traditionally associated with Ephesus and is thought to have been written in the last decade of the first century.

The gospel of John, however, is not simply an eyewitness account, but reveals several stages of composition. Abrupt geographical, chronological and literary transitions, as well as duplication of narrative material, suggest sources that were worked into the final composition. For example, there is the addition of chs 15-17 and 21 after what appear to be formal conclusions in 14:31 and 20:30-31. The Prologue (1:1-18) seems to have been an early hymn, now suitably tailored to serve as an introduction to the gospel. These difficulties among others have led to various theories about sources and editions. Since we are concerned with the gospel in its present form, these theories need not concern us for, in spite of difficulties, the final composition reads as a coherent and profound narrative.

In the community of the Beloved Disciple[18] the gospel tradition was shaped in the light of liturgical, catechetical, polemical and apologetical needs of the community. The discourses were developed from the sayings of Jesus following the pattern of

17. Ireneus (d 202 AD) cites Polycarp (d 156 AD) among his sources. Many scholars today have difficulty accepting this identification and think that there was some confusion or obscuring of the tradition.
18. Cf R. Brown, *The Community of the Beloved Disciple,* New York: Paulist Press, 1979

personified Wisdom's speeches in the Old Testament. The deeds of Jesus were worked into highly dramatic scenes followed by discourses to explain their significance. Thus the Jesus tradition has been transformed and made transparent in its christological viewpoint. The theme of the gospel is focused on Jesus' 'hour' of glorification, his return to the Father at the crucifixion. Jesus has been sent to reveal the Father before returning to the 'glory' that he had with the Father. Conflicts over Jesus' identity[19] lead to progressive rejection and death that, paradoxically, is the manifestation of his 'glory.'

The reader of John must be sensitive to his use of symbolic language, irony, misunderstanding and dualistic expressions. For example, the symbols of life, light, and bread point to Jesus as the source of true life for believers. Opponents make statements about Jesus that are sarcastic or derogatory, but are true in a sense not realised by the speaker (e.g. 11:50). The characters that interact with Jesus in the narrative are at different levels of understanding so Jesus is often misunderstood, or what he says is taken in a literal or superficial way. This allows Jesus to explain his teaching more fully (e.g. 2:19-21). A double meaning can often be found in Jesus' sayings. The dialogue partner takes one meaning, whereas Jesus intends another (e.g. 3:3-7). John also makes use of dualistic expressions: light and darkness, above and below, life and death, etc. These expressions throw light on the process of division that is taking place within the story. There is no middle ground between belief and unbelief.

OUTLINE

The structure of the gospel consists of a Prologue, an independent hymn suitably adapted, which encapsulates the major

19. The long controversy between Jesus and his opponents in ch 7-8 is interrupted by the story of the woman taken in adultery. Many ancient manuscripts place this story after 7:36 or 21:25, while others place it after Lk 21:38 or 24:53. Others omit it altogether. It appears to have been an early free-floating unit of tradition that has now in its present location become part of the canonical collection.

themes and motifs of the gospel. It is followed by the Book of Signs (ch 1-12) which depicts Jesus' public ministry. Jesus performs a number of wondrous deeds that are interpreted for the reader in the discourses. He engages in discussion with opponents and crowds, and moves freely between Galilee and Judea. The Book of Glory is restricted to discussion with the disciples alone and it interprets the significance of the paschal events (ch 13-17). This is followed by the passion and resurrection narratives (ch 18-20). An Epilogue then narrates more appearances of the risen Christ (ch 21). The whole gospel is a progressive manifestation of the glory of the Son of God who has come from above to reveal the Father and returns again.

Prologue: A preview of the gospel. Jesus is the pre-existent and incarnate Word who has come to reveal God to us (1:1-18)

I Book of Signs: The Word reveals himself to his own, but they do not accept him (1:19-12:50)

(a) Initial revelation of Jesus to the disciples: John the Baptist's testimony, acknowledgement by first disciples (1:19-51)

(b) From Cana and back to Cana (2:1-4:54): themes of replacement and newness; water into wine, cleansing and replacement of Temple, new birth (Nicodemus), John's final witness, new worship (Samaritan woman), new life (healing of official's son)

(c) Replacement of Jewish feasts (5:1-10:40): sabbath rest replaced (5:1-47); Passover, bread of life replaces manna (6:1-71); Tabernacles, Jesus replaces water and light ceremonies (7:1-10:21); Dedication, Jesus replaces Temple altar (10:22-42)

(d) Lazarus is raised to life while Jesus is condemned to death; Jesus is anointed for burial, enters Jerusalem, end of public ministry, coming of his 'hour', recapitulation (11:1-12:50)

II Book of Glory: To those who accept him Jesus reveals his glory by returning to the Father through death, resurrection, ascension and coming of the Spirit (13:1-20:31)

(a) The Last Supper and discourse: meal, washing of disciples' feet, Judas' betrayal, introduction to discourse, Peter's denial foretold (13:1-38); the last discourse; departure of Jesus, in-dwelling, the Advocate, allegory of the vine and branches, the world's hatred, the coming of the Advocate (14:1-16:33); the prayer of Jesus (17:1-26)

(b) Passion and death: arrest, Jesus before Annas and Caiaphas, trial before Pilate, crucifixion, death, burial (18:1-19:42)

(c) Resurrection: empty tomb, appearances to Mary of Magdala, disciples and Thomas, conclusion (20:1-31)

Epilogue: Resurrection appearances in Galilee; to seven disciples, Jesus and Peter, the Beloved Disciple, conclusion (21:1-25)

STORYLINE

The Prologue is a hymn that informs us about the identity of Jesus. He is the Word, a divine Being, true light and bringer of life, Word made flesh, the Messiah, the only Son of the Father who is God's Revealer. Not recognised by the world and rejected by his own, he empowers all who accept him to become God's children, sharing a fullness that surpasses the Law given by Moses. John the Baptist's role is that of witness. As the story unfolds, Jesus' identity will be confirmed both by what he says and what he does.

In a pattern of days, the narrator shows the gradual recognition of who Jesus is. John the Baptist explains his own role and hails Jesus as the Lamb of God and some of his disciples follow Jesus. Various titles are conferred on Jesus: Messiah, the one described in the Law and the Prophets, Teacher, Son of God, King of Israel, Son of Man and Jesus is the one who promises 'greater things' to those who follow him. At Cana Jesus provides wine for the wedding feast. This is seen as replacing the water used for Jewish ritual washings and fulfilling the Old Testament promises of abundance of wine in messianic times. Thus Jesus reveals his glory and his disciples believe in him. He goes up to Jerusalem for Passover and confronts the moneychangers in the Temple. In cleansing the Temple, Jesus is replacing its function, although the full implications will be grasped only after the resurrection. Many believe because of the signs he performs, but lack true understanding.

Nicodemus is a representative of this kind of faith. Although a rabbi, he cannot grasp the idea of spiritual rebirth and that Jesus is the source of life. Dialogue becomes monologue as Jesus explains that he must be lifted up to become the source of eternal life for believers. Yet people prefer to hide their evil ways rather than live in the truth. John the Baptist again witnesses to Jesus as his mission is ending and the narrator draws the chapter to a close with a summary. Jesus' conversation with the Samaritan woman takes place during a trip to Galilee. The encounter is described in a series of scenes. In the course of conversation the woman, in spite of initial misunderstanding, gradually comes to recognise who Jesus is. As she departs to share her discovery with the townspeople, Jesus is in dialogue with the disciples about mission and harvest as large numbers of Samaritans converge on Jesus and acknowledge him as Saviour of the world. The healing of the official's son that follows underscores the link between believing and having life as the official and his household come to faith in Jesus.

The second journey to Jerusalem is the setting for the first overt opposition to Jesus provoked by the healing of the crippled man on the sabbath. The narrative that follows exposes the real issue as being Jesus' claim to equality with God. Jesus defends his claim to give life and to judge, which are divine prerogatives, by appealing to the special relationship he enjoys with God. Five witnesses are advanced as testimony and Jesus warns that the Jews' confidence in Moses is misplaced, for Moses himself will condemn them. At Passover time, Jesus feeds the hungry crowd, walks on the water, and delivers a discourse on the bread of life. Traditional material is shaped into a lengthy discourse on Jesus as the bread of life come down from heaven. His words together with the eucharistic Bread are the source of eternal life which establish a special relationship between him and the believer. Jesus nourishes his followers through word and sacrament. Yet many disciples turn away and Jesus is left with the Twelve, one of whom will betray him, while Peter makes a profession of faith.

When Jesus goes up to Jerusalem for Tabernacles, there is a lengthy debate between him and the people as to his identity, and this provokes a division among them. Using the symbolism of water and light associated with the feast, Jesus announces that from within himself will flow rivers of living water, i.e. the Spirit. This is followed by the theme of Jesus as light of the world. The situation turns hostile as various charges are hurled against Jesus, ending in an attempt to stone him. Jesus speaks in a symbolic way that is misunderstood by the crowd and predicts that when he gives his life for others, they will recognise that Jesus bears the divine name 'I am'. Therefore, those who seek to stone Jesus cannot be true descendants of Abraham and are branded instead as children of the devil. The story of the woman taken in adultery is a later insertion. It vividly depicts Jesus' graciousness and mercy towards the woman and it is easy to see why the church wished to make a place for it in the gospel.

The story of the man born blind is a highly dramatic narrative that shows a movement from sight to insight as the blind man who has recovered his sight from Jesus, the light of the world, comes to recognise more clearly who he is. The increasing hostility and blindness of his interrogators is contrasted with the blind man's growing perceptiveness. It ends ironically with those who claim to see becoming blind. By means of the allegory of the shepherd and the sheep, Jesus further clarifies his role and characterises his opponents as hirelings, robbers and wolves. In contrast, Jesus is the true shepherd who calls his sheep by name and lays down his life for them. On the feast of Dedication which celebrated God's presence with his people, Jesus claims to be the one consecrated by God and sent into the world. Offended by his claim to equality with God, opponents try to stone him and have him arrested.

The raising of Lazarus brings to a climax the signs of Jesus when he declares that he is the resurrection and the life. Yet this declaration ironically leads to a decision on the part of the

Jewish authorities to have him put to death. Jesus is anointed for burial at Bethany, enters Jerusalem in triumph and is acclaimed King of Israel. The arrival of the Greeks signals the coming of his 'hour' when, like a grain of wheat, he must die to bear fruit. His public ministry ends with the narrator observing that although the light has come into the world, many chose to remain in darkness, thereby fulfilling Isaiah's prediction.

The Book of Glory consists of a lengthy discourse wherein Jesus prepares 'his own' who accept him for the ordeal to come, as well as for future life in the community of his followers. The footwashing scene symbolises the kind of loving 'service' Jesus is about to perform in his death, thereby setting an example for his disciples. As Judas departs to betray him, the Beloved Disciple is mentioned for the first time. Jesus issues a new commandment to love 'as I have loved you'. The discourse consists of diverse and duplicate material that refers to the disciples' grief at Jesus' departure, his return and the coming of the Paraclete. Jesus will return as an indwelling presence in the disciples together with the Father, and he becomes the way, the truth and the life for all who believe. The allegory of the vine and the branches encourages disciples to remain united with Jesus and one another in the face of the world's hostility and persecution. The discourse ends with the prayer of Jesus wherein he prays for his own glorification, for those whom the Father has given him, and for future generations of believers. The timeless character of the discourse gives it an abiding significance. It is cast in the format of Old Testament farewell speeches in which the speaker announces his imminent departure and urges his listeners to hold fast when he is gone.

John's account of the passion and death of Jesus that follows is close to the synoptic outline. The arrest of Jesus in the garden shows him in full control of his destiny. He is interrogated by Annas and Caiaphas, the High Priest, while Peter denies him. The trial before Pilate is a highly developed dramatic scene in seven episodes. Pilate goes in and out between Jesus and the Jews until he passes the death sentence on Jesus whom he had declared innocent. The impression given is that it is really Pilate who is on trial before Jesus over whom he has no real power. Throughout Jesus remains in complete control, he freely lays down his life for others. In the crucifixion, death and burial scenes, Pilate has Jesus proclaimed as the King of the Jews, and Jesus fulfils the scriptures demonstrating that everything is in accordance with God's plan. The mother of Jesus and the Beloved Disciple are brought into a mother-and-son relationship. Jesus departs to the Father, his mission is accomplished and he is buried like a king.

The appearances of the risen Christ take place in Jerusalem. Jesus gives the disciples a mission as he breathes on them to impart the Spirit with power to forgive sins. The gospel ends with the highest christological confession in the gospel as Thomas confesses 'My Lord and my God', and John states his purpose in writing the gospel. The Epilogue has resurrection appearances in Galilee. Peter inherits the role of Jesus as shepherd and the Beloved Disciple, who established the Johannine tradition, is identified as the one who stands behind the gospel tradition.

JESUS IN JOHN'S GOSPEL

The Narrative as a Whole

John's gospel opens with the Prologue in which the identity of Jesus is revealed as God's Word made flesh. The rest of the narrative must be understood in the light of this. It sets Jesus in eternity before the Word was made flesh. Before creation the Word was already with God, indeed was God. All things were made through him. The Word was life and light for human beings. Readers, then, will not be surprised by Jesus' bold claims throughout the gospel as he reveals what he has seen and heard in God's presence. John the Baptist is his witness and the conflict between the Word and the world is foreshadowed. Although the Word came to his own, those who were his own did not receive him. Those who did embrace him became children of God as a result of Jesus' ministry. The Word became flesh and lived among us as God's perfect revelation to the world which beheld his glory in the signs and works that he performed. This is the glory that identifies Jesus as the only-begotten Son of the Father. The content of the Prologue may be summarised as 'revelation'. Jesus is the perfect revelation of God and that is why he is identified with the Word of God. The reader is thus prepared for a narrative in which Jesus will present himself as the revealer from God. The content of the Prologue is illumined by the narrative.

The story opens with the witness of John the Baptist who identifies Jesus as the Lamb of God who takes away the sin of the world and testifies that he saw the Spirit descend and remain upon Jesus. Having seen this, John now testifies that Jesus is the Son of God. Two disciples call Jesus 'rabbi' and accept his invitation to come and see where he lives. Another disciple, Andrew, testifies that they have found the Messiah and Philip declares that they have found him about whom Moses in the Law and the prophets wrote. Nathaniel confesses that Jesus is the Son of God and king of Israel. Jesus assures him that he will see the heavens open and the angels of God ascending and descending on the Son of Man. Already various titles have identified Jesus of Nazareth, but in the light of the Prologue these traditional titles take on a new meaning.

Jesus begins his ministry at Cana where he performs the first of his signs and reveals his glory. In Jerusalem, he cleanses the Temple, thereby replacing it, and performs more signs. Nicodemus comes to him and on the basis of the signs acknowledges that Jesus has come from God, but does not grasp the significance of Jesus' identity. The story of the Samaritan woman leads the reader to further clarification of Jesus' identity. He is acknowledged as a prophet and identifies himself as the Messiah. The woman's testimony leads the Samaritans' declaration that Jesus is the Saviour of the world. Having returned to Galilee he heals the official's son. In the first part of the Johannine narrative various titles identify Jesus. He reveals God's glory and is the new locus of worship and source of life.

He is the prophet-Messiah and Saviour of the world. He is the Son of Man who has descended from heaven and will return to God when he is lifted up on the cross. The narrator explains that God 'sent' his Son into the world as light of the world, not to condemn, but to save it. Furthermore, Jesus testifies to what he has seen and heard because he comes from above.

Debates between Jesus and the Jews take up the major portion of chapters 5-10. The nature of the relationship between Jesus and God becomes the central issue. The Jews dispute with Jesus because he makes himself equal to God (5:18; cf 10:33). The first debate is occasioned by the sabbath healing in Jerusalem and points to Jesus as Son of the Father who has been sent with authority to give life and to judge, as the ensuing discourse discloses. Jesus affirms that he works on the sabbath because his Father works. This suggests that Jesus is in some way equal to God because the Father has shown him all things and given him authority to do what he does – to give life and to judge.

In the discourse following the multiplication of the loaves, he explains that the Father offers us Jesus himself as the true bread from heaven. Whoever eats this bread will never die. Jesus, the Word incarnate, is the bread of life who has given his flesh for the life of the world. This claim is followed by a further one on the feast of Tabernacles that Jesus is the light of the world because he reveals the Father. To his opponents who have been questioning Jesus' origins and messiahship, it is an occasion for further debate about Jesus' identity. Jesus speaks about going where the Jews cannot come and when they have lifted up the Son of Man, they will realise who he is. The discourse ends with Jesus declaring: 'Before Abraham was, I am' (8:58). He is also the good shepherd who lays down his life for his sheep. Jesus' claims, however, do not satisfy the Jews and so on the feast of Dedication they ask him to tell them plainly if he is the Messiah. When Jesus affirms this and adds that he and the Father are one, the Jews accuse him of blasphemy. The Messiah is the one who comes from God, the pre-existent Word, the Son whom the Father has sent into the world.

The last and greatest sign, the raising of Lazarus, reveals Jesus as the resurrection and the life. Yet the Pharisees and chief priests convene a council and the High Priest declares that it is better for one man to die than the whole nation perish. Aware of his impending death, he accepts an anointing and enters Jerusalem as King of Israel. When the Greeks ask to see him, he knows that this is the hour in which the Son of Man is glorified and promises that when he is lifted up, he will draw all people to himself.

In the first half of the gospel, John presents Jesus as the new tabernacle (1:14), new Temple (2:21), as one who replaces the waters of Jewish purification (2:1-12) and the locus of Jewish worship (4:21-24). In chapters five to ten, the figure of Jesus is interpreted against the backdrop of the Jewish feasts of Passover, Tabernacles and Dedication and the symbolism associated with these feasts is transferred to Jesus. All this is meant to tell us something about Jesus *vis-à-vis* Israel. Jesus embodies all the significance that the Old Testament institutions and feasts embodied. They are not so much fulfilled as replaced. Jesus now becomes living bread, living water, the light of the world and the lamb who takes away the sin of the world. In Jesus the offer of life, dimly present in Old Testament worship with its ritual, is definitively offered. He is 'the resurrection and the life,' and people are judged on the basis of their response to him.

In the second half of the narrative, Jesus delivers a farewell discourse to the disciples who believe in him. Jesus speaks of his origin and destiny as he develops the theme of departure and return to the Father. It is clear that Jesus' death is not one of humiliation and defeat, but one of exaltation and glorification because he is returning to the Father when he is lifted up on the cross. With the Father he will prepare a place for the disciples and will send the Paraclete. To Thomas' complaint that they do not know where Jesus is going, Jesus declares: 'I am the way, the truth, and the life' (14:6). When Philip asks Jesus to show them the Father, Jesus replies that to see him is to see the Father (14:9). Jesus employs the image of the vine to explain the intimate relationship between himself, the Father and the disciples (15:1-8).

In chapter 18 the evangelist returns to the historical events of Jesus' arrest, the hearings, the trial before Pilate, the crucifixion and resurrection. The trial before Pilate is so described that the majesty and dignity of Jesus is prominent. Accused as King of the Jews, Jesus confesses his royalty but reinterprets it, not in worldly terms, but as the power given him to testify to the truth (18:36-37). The climax comes in 19:12-16 when Pilate presents Jesus as king and the chief priests respond: 'We have no king but Caesar' (19:15). Jesus is in control right up to the end, even his death completes the work the Father has given him to do (cf 19:30).

For John the heart of Jesus' revelation is his cross and resurrection. His being 'lifted up' refers simultaneously to being raised up on the cross and to his enthronement as a royal figure, Christ the King, with the ironic title 'King of the Jews' (19:19) placed over his head at the behest of Pilate. The kingly posture of Jesus during the trial scene, the voluntary handing over of his life and his lavish burial, all point to Jesus' royal status. It is the hour of Jesus' 'glorification' (cf 12:23, 17:1, 5), the act by which God's presence is manifested to the world and the true identity of the Son of Man is revealed. The gospel fittingly comes to an end with the climactic confession of Thomas: 'My Lord and my God' (20:28).

Titles of Jesus

At the heart of the gospel stands the figure of Jesus of whom a variety of images and expressions are predicated to express the relationship between Jesus and God, and Jesus and human beings. John uses traditional titles and adds new ones, in particular, Jesus as the Word or Revealer of the Father.[20] The presentation of Jesus is more symbolic than literal, yet Jesus is no mere cipher or mythical figure. Although Jesus is God's Word, he is also 'made flesh' (1:14). He experiences fatigue (4:6) and anguish (12:27, 13:21). He weeps at the death of Lazarus, his friend (11:33-35), shows irritation (2:4) and suspicion (2:24). Jesus con-

20. Cf R. Schnackenburg, *Jesus in the Gospels*, pp 247-294

verses with real people – Nicodemus, the Samaritan woman, the paralytic, the man born blind. His friends are Martha, Mary and his disciples. He enters into controversy with opponents.

Yet Jesus is more than a human figure in John. What is often only implicit or hinted at in the synoptics is made explicit. It may be said that the whole structure of the gospel circles around the figure of Jesus. He is the one who has descended from heaven and ascends again (cf 3:13, 6:62). Everything is revealed on the basis of his having been with God, his pre-existence. In John there is a perceptible shift from the earthly, crucified and risen Jesus to the one who comes from God and works together with him in the world for the salvation of humans. The narrator wishes to portray Jesus as God's Word and Wisdom incarnate throughout the gospel in a way that goes well beyond the synoptics. Realising that God's Son, the Word, Wisdom itself, has come down from heaven and returned again is the key, not only to understanding Jesus' identity, but his whole ministry as well. The historical background is presupposed and even accessible with some of the details that John provides.

Already in 1:19-51 John has gathered together a number of traditional titles. Messiah is mentioned frequently because he wishes to emphasise that Jesus is the expected Messiah. Yet John has profoundly redefined it. The Messiah is the one who comes from above, whom God has sent into the world. Jesus is Messiah, not because he is of David's lineage and born in Bethlehem, but because he is God's Word made flesh. The gospel transcends any expectations linked to traditional messianic hopes. John's christology is more than an expansion of possibilities already present in Jewish and early Christian sources. He uses categories formerly used of the transcendent reality of God to describe the earthly career of Jesus. With the introduction of the Word in the Prologue, John brings in the notion of pre-existence of Jesus with God. In 1:18 he links the Word and Son christologies, and by referring to Jesus' return to the glory he had with the Father before creation (cf 17:5, 24), he succeeds in linking the pre-existent Word with the Jesus of the narrative. In this way John sets the parameters for an incarnational christology. We will look at the titles for Jesus unique to John and traditional ones he has developed in a special way.

One Sent. Fundamental to John's christology is the origin of Jesus. He is the pre-existent Word who has become flesh and dwelt amongst us. If the origin of Jesus is in God, then his presence in history is the result of his having 'been sent' by the Father. Jesus is the special envoy sent with the authority of the sender. His mission from the Father is what validates the claims he makes (cf 17:21). No human being has ever seen God, yet one person is able to reveal him – the one who comes from the Father (cf 1:18, 6:46). In the Johannine worldview such a mission involves the descent of the Revealer from above (cf 3:13), and his subsequent ascent to where he was before (6:62). 'The Father who sent me' (5:37, 6:44) is a favourite formula used by Jesus which connects his being sent with the Father as sender. The two verbs to send *(pempein, apostellein)* are used some forty two times to designate God's Son being sent into the world: 'For God so loved the world that he gave his only Son, so that whoever believes in him may not perish but may have eternal life' (3:16).

More than the prophets who preceded him as messengers from God, Jesus is the true bearer of life sent into the world of humans to rescue them, a light in the darkness of a world that has become estranged from God (cf 1:4-5). He came to lead them to God and give them life in abundance (cf 10:10). With a plethora of images and symbols this new life coming from God is described: a spring of living water welling up to eternal life (4:14), the bread that endures forever (6:27), the light that dispels the darkness of sin (8:12), the resurrection and the life (11:25-26). Through the gift of life given by the one sent by God there is the possibility of new life and the way to God is opened up (cf 14:6-7). Jesus is sent from the realm of God to lead everyone to it. Those who believe the one sent from God become children of God (1:12), are born from above (3:3), and are filled with the Spirit (cf 7:39). This life coming from God, through Jesus, is the answer to the question of human existence and its meaning.

Son. The one sent into the world by the Father is the Son who stands in a special relationship to God. Central to the revealing mission of Jesus is his being Son of God. This title was already in the tradition, but John also uses the absolute term, 'the Son,' some twenty times throughout the narrative and it is almost exclusive to him. The Son is not simply a title of Christ, but one that stands out above other predicates to show Christ's unique relationship to God, 'the Father who sent me'. This relationship of Son to Father provides a rich bond that binds them together. The Father loves the Son (3:35), just as the Son loves the Father (14:31), so much so that the Son can do nothing by himself, but only speaks and does what he has seen and learned from the Father (cf 5:19, 8:28). There is a functional union between Father and Son (5:19), but also some identity of being: 'The Father and I are one' (10:30). This oneness is so close that Jesus' words and works are those of his Father (12:50, 14:10). Through his words and works, indeed through his entire person, the Son reveals the Father so completely that to see him is to see the Father: 'Whoever has seen me has seen the Father' (14:9). This familiarity between Father and Son is based on the fact that already in his pre-existence the Son has been close to the Father: 'My glory which you have given me because you loved me before the foundation of the world' (17:24). This close relationship continues throughout Jesus' earthly career. The formula 'I am in the Father, and the Father is in me' (10:38, cf 14:10-11, 17:21) maintains both the distinction of persons and the unity that exists between them. Since Jesus is close to the Father's heart (1:18), he shares in the divinity of God (1:2). To underline the uniqueness of the Son, John uses 'only-begotten' (1:14, 18, 3:16, 18) and Jesus is given functions that hitherto had been reserved to God alone – to give life and to judge (cf 5:21-22).

As well, Jesus uses filial language to express his relationship to God. He works as his Father works: 'Truly, truly, I tell you, the Son can do nothing on his own, but only what he sees the Father doing; for whatever he does, the Son does likewise' (5:19). It is as the Father's Son that he renders judgement: 'I can do nothing on my own; as I hear, I judge; and my judgement is just, because I seek to do not my own will, but the will of him who sent me' (5:30). This relationship between Father and Son is also one of great intimacy: '… that they may be one. As you, Father, are in me and I am in you' (17:21). In his human activity Jesus reveals himself as the obedient Son; his whole life is one of obedient service for the sake of others and so he becomes a source of new life for them (cf 12:24). Yet the Father is greater than the Son (14:28), thereby preserving the priority of the Father as the one who sends and Jesus in his human nature as the one sent.

Son of Man. This title is used in two of the three associations it has in the synoptics. John uses this traditional term to present the earthly ministry of Jesus as the locus where Jesus, the Son of Man, reveals God and thus brings life and judgement. But John draws the synoptic judgement function of the Son of Man at the parousia back into the historical encounter with Jesus, although the future judgement is not totally excluded (5:28-29). In John the title is never used to refer to the one who will come in the clouds of heaven. The second use of the term is in connection with Jesus' being lifted up on the cross. This predominant use is within the pattern of descent and ascent. The Son of Man will be lifted up in his crucifixion: 'Just as Moses lifted up the serpent in the wilderness, so must the Son of Man be lifted up' (3:14, cf 8:28). But the Son of Man is the one who has already descended from heaven and so is uniquely qualified to reveal things 'from above': 'No one has ascended into heaven, except the one who descended from heaven, the Son of Man' (3:13, cf 3:31-32). So then when the Son of Man is lifted up, he returns to where he was before (cf 6:62). His death on the cross, although externally the hour of darkness and defeat, is in reality the hour of Jesus' departure out of this world to the Father (13:1). The Son of Man is also the means of communication between heaven and earth: 'Truly, truly, I tell you, you will see heaven opened and the angels of God ascending and descending on the Son of Man' (1:51). The Son of Man is the one who brings eternal life for those who

partake of his flesh and blood in the eucharist and gives partici-
pants full communion with himself by abiding in them: 'Truly,
truly, I tell you, unless you eat the flesh of the Son of Man and
drink his blood, you have no life in you ... Whoever eats my
flesh and drinks my blood abides in me and I in him ... The one
who eats this bread will live forever' (6:53, 56, 58).

In John, the Son of Man is a figure shaped by Christian faith,
a real, living human being, Jesus of Nazareth. He is the one who
comes from God and who is exalted and glorified when lifted up
on the cross.

Lamb of God. Jesus is the Lamb of God (1:29, 36) 'who takes
away the sin of the world'. The background for this designation
may be the paschal lamb (cf 1 Cor 5:7; 1 Pet 1:19). In John 19:36
Jesus' legs are not broken, an obvious reference to the paschal
lamb, and Jesus dies on the day of preparation for the Passover
when the lambs were being slaughtered in the Temple. There
may be a reference to the offering of Isaac, the beloved son,
whom Abraham was bidden to offer up in sacrifice (Gen 22:1-
19). Jesus is also the good shepherd who lays down his life for
his sheep (10:11, 15). The symbol 'Lamb of God' seems to have
been created by the evangelist out of Christian experience and
reflection.

I Am. A unique feature of Johannine christology are statements made by Jesus using 'I am'. In some passages Jesus speaks
figuratively and this tells us something about his role *vis-à-vis*
human beings. He identifies himself with something already
known to the hearers. In all of them, beneath the metaphors, is
the claim that he is the source of life that comes from God. Thus
Jesus, after the multiplication of the loaves, declares: 'I am the
bread of life' (6:35, 51) which truly offers eternal life, unlike the
manna in the desert which the fathers ate. Jesus is the genuine
bread because he descends from God and offers the life that
comes from God (6:33). At the feast of Tabernacles Jesus says: 'I
am the light of the world' (8:12, 9:5). Before his coming people
lived in darkness. Now that Jesus brings the revelation of God
which unmasks the world for what it is, people can distinguish

the light from the darkness and so a choice can be made (cf 3:19ff).

Additional 'I am' statements emphasise the relationship between Jesus and his followers. Unlike thieves and robbers who destroy the sheep, Jesus announces: 'I am the door of the sheepfold' (10:7). Those who enter by him will be safe and will be given life. Jesus also adds: 'I am the good shepherd' (10:11). Unlike the hireling who has no care for the sheep, Jesus lays down his life for them. Jesus is 'the genuine vine' (15:1), the true source of life for his followers. Cut off from him they wither and die, but those who remain joined to him bear fruit. He is 'the resurrection and the life' (11:25). Those who believe in him will never die, but will live with God's life. Finally, Jesus is 'the way, the truth, and the life' (14:6). Nobody comes to the Father except through him. Jesus leads the way to genuine life that comes from God.

All these declarations are closely associated with Jesus' role, what Jesus is in relation to humans. He is bread, light, sheepgate, true shepherd, resurrection and life, the way, the truth and the life, and the genuine vine. He is the source of life for humans (vine, resurrection and life), and the means through whom people find life (way, door, shepherd), revealing to them the truth (truth) and nourishing their life (bread). Many of these metaphors were already used in the Old Testament to describe God's relationship to Israel.

In other passages the phrase 'I am' has a solemn and sacral use similar to that found in the Old Testament for the divine name (cf 4:26, 6:20, 8:24, 28, 58, 13:19). The dramatic impact of the phrase is suggested at Jesus' arrest. When his captors are told 'I am' he (Jesus), they fall to the ground (18:6). Some light is thrown on this incident by the disputation in 8:12-58 in which 'I am' occurs three times (8:24, 28, 58). In the last of these, Jesus' opponents recognise the deeper implications of the statement by their attempt to stone him for blasphemy. Later on they want to stone him because 'being a human being, you make yourself God' (10:33).

This is precisely what the absolute use of the phrase 'I am' would suggest in the light of the Old Testament. In Exodus 3:14 it is used in the self-identification of God to Moses. When the prophet of the exile, Deutero-Isaiah, wishes to assert the author- itative word of Yahweh, the God of Israel, over against the claims of other gods, he uses the Hebrew expressions 'I am he', 'I am Yahweh' (cf Is 41:4, 43:10, 13, 45:18, 46:5, 48:12). This was translated in the Greek version as 'I am' *(ego eimi)*, the same phrase used in John. Just as in Second Isaiah God is revealed through this formula, so also John reveals the uniqueness of Jesus by appropriating it and applying it to Jesus. To frightened disciples crossing the lake, Jesus assures them: 'I am, do not be afraid' (6:20). Similarly the collapse of the soldiers when Jesus says 'I am (he)' (18:6) suggests that Jesus is someone more than a human being. He is one who brings comfort and strength to frightened disciples and evokes awe and reverence from his captors. For John, Jesus is God manifested in the flesh.

Word. This term is found only in the Prologue. With God before creation, the Word was involved as an active agent in creation, but the focus is on the world of people for whom the Word is light and life, but from whom people have inexplicably turned away. The Word became incarnate and lived among peo- ple to bring the revelation of the true God and lead them to full- ness of life. The Word became 'flesh,' i.e. earthly, limited, frail and transitory, all that is typical of being human. There is no doubt that John has in mind a real human being, Jesus of Nazareth, who appeared in history to reveal the divine 'glory,' i.e. the felt presence of a loving, saving and guiding God in the Old Testament, now made visible in Jesus Christ. We must look at the story of Jesus as related by John to see how his glory is made visible at Cana (2:11), at the raising of Lazarus (11:4, 40), but especially at Jesus' death on the cross, his hour of glory. In John the divinity of Jesus is derived from his pre-existence, and in his becoming flesh, divinity and humanity are united in his person, thus pre-empting all forms of mythical thinking.

Although the term Word disappears after the Prologue, what

follows is an elaboration of Word christology. Jesus is the one who has fully and definitively revealed the true God and revelation is the central theme of John's narrative. To see and hear him is to see and hear the Father. Accordingly, 'Word' is an appropriate concept to express the significance of Jesus and his ministry. Just as the human word reveals something of the person who utters it, so too Jesus reveals the Father who sent him. Jesus is not a second God, but God incarnate, God making himself present to human beings within the confines of human experience. Based on the incarnation of the Word, John has sketched his portrait of Christ. He begins not with the human Jesus, but with the divine Word which becomes a human being of flesh and blood. In this way the evangelist does justice to both the divinity and humanity of Jesus.

Jesus as Word richly associates him with the Old Testament and Jewish traditions. From the opening chapters of Genesis, John borrows the words 'in the beginning', creation, light, darkness and life. From the Sinai theophany narrative in Exodus come the words tabernacle, glory and enduring love. The activity of the word in creation and in the history of salvation, especially the dynamic word of the Lord in the prophetic literature (cf Is 56:10-11) and in the psalms also finds an echo in the Prologue. The various attributes and activities ascribed to the word of God, wisdom and Law are now ascribed to the Word, especially those of personified Wisdom (cf Prov 8:22-31; Sir 24; Baruch 3-4; Wis 7-9). Both Word and Wisdom are with God from the beginning; both are involved in the creation of the world; both seek a place to dwell among humans; both are within the Jewish tradition of speculation on the early chapters of Genesis; both are partially identified with the Law. All these strands are woven together in John's concept of the Word. With the incarnation of the Word, though, John goes beyond the idea of a pre-existent spiritual power that is operative in the world whether as word, wisdom or Law. None of these were ever before identified with a human being. It is not the Law, but Jesus Christ who is now the source of light and life. The tabernacling presence of God among his people is now transferred to the incarnate Word (1:14). The Prologue, therefore, affirms both the pre-existence and the incarnation of the Word.

The term Word has an enormous breadth of meaning. It is associated with the creative and prophetic word of God as well as with wisdom and Law. It is said to be with God (1:1) which suggests both individuality and identification, and that the Word was God (1:2). In this way, John is proclaiming the divinity of Jesus that is reinforced in the course of the narrative. To see and know him is to see and know the Father (cf 8:19, 14:9). Jesus is the one in whom humans encounter the full revelation of God because he is fully identified with God (cf 1:18). Based on the pattern of personified Wisdom's descent and return, the gospel narrative tells the story of the Word incarnate who fulfils the Father's mission to reveal him, to take away the sins of the world, and empower believers to become children of God. This is the perspective that dominates the whole appearance and activity of Jesus during his earthly existence. His entire ministry is understood in the light of his coming from God and his return. In this way, John articulates a christology that surpasses the synoptics, one that is incarnational as well as paschal.

On the basis of the paradox of the incarnation of the Word certain tensions within the narrative are clarified. On the one hand, the Son of God is as close as possible to the Father and equal to him, yet he freely submits himself to the will of the Father even to death. He is the Word working with God from the beginning; it can be said that he is in the Father and the Father is in him (14:10-11). Since the Word became flesh and was sent into the world as a human being, his subordination to the Father can be understood: 'The Father is greater than I' (14:28). The peculiar combination of exaltation and glorification that we find in the passion account is also based on the incarnation. In his trial and passion the majesty of the one who comes from above shines out and it is from the dying body of Jesus that redeeming streams of blood and water flow (cf 19:34), so that people will look on the one they have pierced (19:34). The resurrection reveals Jesus as the living one who is ascending to the Father again (cf 20:16-17), and it is Jesus' glorified body which still bears the traces of the crucifixion that is the source of the Spirit for the disciples (cf 20:20-29).

All this implies that Jesus is divine (cf 1:1, 20:28). More so than the synoptics, John brings the divinity of Jesus to the fore, thus making explicit what was at least implicit during Jesus' ministry and corresponding to the experience of early Christians. Clearly Jesus gave the impression of one who has a unique relationship to God not shared by other previous emissaries. What he passed on was an implicit and indirect impression of that relationship. It took time for the unfolding and explication of it to reach the high level of articulation that we find in John. The understanding of Jesus as divine, already expressed in a variety of ways in earlier traditions, has come to full clarity in John. Jesus is the one in whom God is seen by humans and in whom God's salvation is concretised in a totally new way. Jesus is the presence of God among mortals, he replaces and surpasses the institutions of Judaism that mediated God's presence to his people.

CHAPTER SIX

The Historical Jesus

INTRODUCTION

If there is no traceable connection between the Jesus of history and the glorified Lord of the gospels, Christianity runs the risk of becoming a myth. Christian faith demands that there be an identity between the Jesus who walked the roads of Palestine and the Christ of faith, the exalted Lord of the gospels. Today, after more than two hundred years of research into the Jesus of history, with widely divergent and often contradictory results, there is a greater willingness on the part of exegetes to attribute a more explicit christology to Jesus during his lifetime. And so a continuity between the lifetime of Jesus and the gospel portrait of him may well be more inclusive than was formerly thought.

To avoid confusion, some distinctions and clarifications need to be made at the outset. When we speak of the historical Jesus, we have in mind what can be recovered of the life of Jesus of Nazareth by the application of modern scientific method to records written by those who believed that Jesus was God's agent of salvation for humans. It is a scholarly creation based on reading beneath the gospel surface and discarding all interpretation and development that took place in the early church. The validity of the construct depends on the criteria employed.[21] But scholars themselves are divided about the real value of some of the criteria for discerning the historical Jesus. It is also a construct based on limited evidence and tends to produce a minimalist view that all academics can agree on. At the very most, it

21. Five criteria are usually offered: the criteria of embarrassment, dissimilarity, multiple attestation, coherence and rejection. Cf J. P. Meier, *The Marginal Jew: Rethinking the Historical Jesus*, vol 1. New York: Doubleday, 1991, pp 167-195

can only give us a fraction of the detail and colouring of the actual Jesus, i.e. Jesus as he actually was in his lifetime. A portrait of the actual Jesus would involve everything of interest about him, so that he becomes intelligible to others and that his personality can emerge. The results of scholarly investigation is also limited in that it lacks theological and spiritual depth, and reflects what a particular scholar wishes to highlight. It will inevitably change as methods are revised and refined. The gospel Jesus refers to the portrait painted by the evangelists that stems from a select-ive arrangement in narrative form of the Jesus tradition to pro-mote and strengthen faith. The evangelists included information about Jesus which served that purpose, and the needs of the au-dience also affected the content and the presentation. The real Jesus is the one that attracted and convinced the disciples who in turn proclaimed him throughout the world. Major aspects of the real Jesus went unreported and are therefore unknowable. Given that historical investigation excludes on principle any-thing of a religious or theological nature, the historical Jesus is furthest away from giving us an appreciation of the real Jesus. On the other hand, the gospel portraits contain a significant amount of material from the actual Jesus, and is as near as we are ever likely to get to him from the information we are left with.

In popular usage, history is 'what really happened' and is contrasted with the fictional and mythical which are regarded as 'made up'. History is what is true, what is not history is false. But history is the end result of intelligence and imagination, not simply what happened in the past. It is an interpretation of events and of surviving records. History is therefore limited since its knowledge deals only with degrees of probability, not certainty, because of the fragmentary character of all historical evidence. When we speak of historical probability rather than certainty, we refer to the level of confidence we have in the pre-sent state of our knowledge, which rests on our ability to verify statements. This in turn depends on the evidence available. It does not judge whether the event in question really happened, but only what we can know about it.

So little material has survived about Jesus outside the New Testament. Our major source then is the canonical gospels since the rest of the New Testament yields few data about the historical Jesus. The apocryphical gospels[22] at most preserve some sayings of Jesus, and there are some passing references in Jewish and pagan sources from the late first and early second centuries.[23] Now, the gospels were written by believers for believers some forty to sixty years after the death of Jesus by second or third generation authors. Each gospel tells the story of Jesus differently and they even disagree on occasion, e.g. the narrative sequence in the synoptics and John is not the same. They yield a limited amount of information about the life of Jesus and are unconcerned for the most part with the precise temporal sequence of events. The gospels then are narratives of faith that differ among themselves; the principle of arrangement within them is more topical, thematic and geographical than strictly chronological. The kinds of material they contain make historical analysis difficult.

In spite of obvious difficulties, we can still speak with a high degree of probability about the historical existence of Jesus, get some sense of his characteristic activity, as well as the movement deriving from him. The broad pattern of Jesus' life is more or less probable; it becomes much more problematic when we get down to concrete events in his life. Some of these events recorded in the gospels are by definition outside the historian's competence, e.g. the transfiguration, the resurrection. Nevertheless, the gospels offer the best chance of arriving at a genuine historical picture of Jesus of Nazareth. The gospel stories do rest upon the historical events of Jesus' ministry. However, the original events were remembered and retold with post-resurrection insight that enabled fuller recognition of their ultimate meaning,

22. This title refers to non-canonical writings closely related in form or content to the four canonical gospels and date from the second century AD.
23. Josephus, *Antiquities* 20.9.1; Suetonius, *Life of Claudius* 5.25.4; Tacitus, *Annals* 25.44.2-8; Pliny the Younger, *Letter* 10.96.

a recognition that would have been beyond the capabilities of the original witnesses.

The Christian faith is not based on a historical reconstruction of the life of Jesus of Nazareth but on religious claims, on the resurrection of Jesus of Nazareth, who is now with God and shares his divine life through the Holy Spirit with those who believe. The resurrection lifts Jesus beyond space and time, although he is still present to believers in the here and now of life. Christians believe that the truest perspective on the person of Jesus is a post-resurrection one, and that the gospels do provide access to the real Jesus. They do so precisely insofar as they reflect the perception of him given by his post-resurrection existence. There is then a need to recognise realities beyond the grasp of historical method. Nevertheless, historical investigations can and do yield important information about Jesus' ministry, but the nature of the sources does not allow a satisfying reconstruction. What it does offer is fragile and in constant need of revision.

Since the Christian faith is based on the incarnation, it does involve some historical claims about Jesus. Therefore, getting to know Jesus of Nazareth in his historical appearance is a worthwhile project. Knowledge of him assures us that the Jesus we encounter in faith has truly entered our history and lived a human life. It reinforces the belief that God really entered history, became one of us, and saves us by leading us in a genuinely human life. Insofar as theology is faith seeking understanding, the quest for the historical Jesus remains an important part of theological reflection. As well, our cultural climate today is marked by an explicit historical consciousness and so this quest gives concrete content to christological statements. Otherwise there is the ever-present danger that Jesus will evaporate into a timeless gnostic or mythic symbol. This search serves to reaffirm the incarnation: 'The Word became flesh and lived among us' (Jn 1:14). It helps to guard against an overemphasis on the divinity of Jesus while playing down or ignoring his humanity. To discover what can be known of Jesus as an historical person also guards against the acknowledgement of him as Messiah and Son of God being reduced to some kind of irrational fideism. The early church did want to pass on what Jesus proclaimed and taught, and did so following the mandate of the resurrected Christ (cf Mt 28:20). There is then descriptive historical knowledge about Jesus of Nazareth and faith knowledge of Jesus as Christ and Lord. The quest for the historical Jesus brackets out what is known by faith without, however, denying it.

The historical investigation of the life and person of Jesus of Nazareth is important, and the gospel records, despite limitations, do yield some historical information to enable a partial reconstruction of his life and personality to emerge.

THE JESUS OF HISTORY

Jesus of Nazareth[24] was born towards the end of the reign of Herod the Great (37-4 BC), around 6 BC. His mother was called Mary, his foster-father Joseph through whom Jesus traced his lineage to David. He was probably born in Bethlehem since no other place is suggested,[25] and reared in Nazareth where he spent about thirty years of his life. By profession he was an artisan or carpenter. Since Joseph makes no appearance during Jesus' public life, it is presumed that he had already died. Mary his mother is mentioned as well as brothers and sisters, the latter in a clan-oriented culture would designate relatives. These apparently did not follow him during his public ministry. Jesus did not marry, he remained celibate.

We know nothing of Jesus' formal education. He was addressed as 'rabbi' by people and could read and understand biblical Hebrew. He would ordinarily have spoken Aramaic, since that was the common language of the Galilean people to whom he preached. He may have had some familiarity with Greek which was spoken in Palestine in the first century.

24. Cf J. P. Meier, 'Jesus,' *The New Jerome Biblical Commentary* (R. E. Brown, J. A. Fitzmyer, R. E. Murphy, eds.), London: Chapman, 1990, pp 1316-28.
25. Cf R. Brown, *The Birth of the Messiah*, London: Chapman, 1977, pp 513-16, for a discussion pertaining to this issue.

Apparently there was nothing in the early life or educational background of Jesus to prepare his fellow townspeople for the public career he later undertook, hence their shock and scandal when he returned to speak in their synagogue (cf Mk 6:1-6 and par). Jesus was regarded as an ordinary layman during his earthly life, and this may explain why the priestly and lay aristocracy in Jerusalem played such a large part in bringing him to trial before Pilate.

Some time in 28-29 AD during the reign of Tiberius (14-37 AD), Jesus emerged from the obscurity of village life in Nazareth to undergo baptism from John the Baptist in the river Jordan. Following in the footsteps of the Old Testament prophets, John preached a message calling sinful Israel to repentance and a baptism of water in view of the imminent judgement of God. Some of Jesus' disciples were John's former followers. Jesus launched out on his own, preached a message that emphasised the definitive reign of God that has now come near to save and called for repentance by way of preparation. Faithful to his promises, he said, God was about to establish his definitive rule by bringing back a scattered Israel through his ministry.

Jesus used many oratorical techniques especially from the wisdom and prophetic tradition to drive home his message. Among these was his use of parables, a form of wisdom speech, to challenge sinful Israel to open their eyes and to think for themselves. There was a note of urgency about his preaching, his audience had to decide to immediately risk all in order to accept Jesus' message and become his followers. He preached a radical reversal of values to bring about the new world of the kingdom, something already present in the parables for those who allowed themselves to be challenged.

Jesus associated with 'tax collectors and sinners', the religiously lost or marginalised, and was opposed to the formalism in worship by pious Jews whom he roundly condemned. His message was one of joy and celebration, anticipated in the meals he shared with sinners and other social outcasts. His non-ascetic lifestyle left him vulnerable to be labelled as a 'glutton and wine-drinker' (cf Lk 15:1-3). Jesus' deeds of power were in the service of liberating people from evil in its various manifestations and making people whole again. His extraordinary cures, exorcisms and nature miracles were never denied by his opponents. They attributed them instead to the power of the devil. Jesus' miracles were concrete manifestations of proclaiming and effecting God's triumph over the powers of evil present in human life. They were, at the same time, also signs and partial realisations of the kingdom. Both Jesus' words and deeds affirmed that the reign of God, although its definitive realisation lay in the indefinite future, was already present in and through his ministry.

In the light of his free offer of salvation and forgiveness, Jesus also gave guidelines on how those who had experienced conversion ought to live. While on the whole affirming the Mosaic Law as the expression of God's will, he rejected the countless precepts and ritual observances that had grown up around it. Instead he sought to radicalise the Law by going back to God's original intention and purpose in giving the Law in the first place, and, like the prophets before him, advocated internalisation of the Law by purifying the wellsprings of the heart. Sometimes this radicalisation of the Law deepened and broadened it, at other times it rescinded the letter. Jesus claimed to know directly in what the will of God consisted and solemnly affirmed it. On the positive side, Jesus summed up the Law as the love of God and love of neighbour. His moral teaching was also a sign of the kingdom's power and presence already breaking into human lives.

As a Jew, Jesus had points of contact with almost every aspect of Judaism, but was never totally identified with any of them. This perhaps explains why he did not take sides in the great social and political questions of the day. He had no agenda for the reform of contemporary society, yet his novel attitude on many issues could not but have social implications, e.g. his advocating love of enemies.

Some people accepted Jesus' message of the kingdom wholeheartedly to the extent of leaving home and livelihood to travel with Jesus, listen to his teaching and share in his ministry. Jesus chose some of them directly to be with him. Out of these a special group called the Twelve, symbolising his mission to gather the twelve tribes of Israel, fulfilled the hopes of the prophets and the apocalyptic writers. He did not found a new sect, but wanted to make the Twelve the nucleus of what he was challenging all Israel to be, i.e. the restored people of God in eschatological times. Jesus sent the Twelve on a limited mission to Israel as preparation for their future work. Yet not all who accepted Jesus' message left behind their ordinary means of living. Some instead provided hospitality for Jesus during his visits to Jerusalem over a three year period. Since Jesus saw his mission as primarily to Israel, he did not undertake any mission to the gentiles, but performed exorcisms and healings for them by way of exception. Yet, he said, the gentiles would be included in the great eschatological banquet while unbelieving Jews would be cast out.

The core of Jesus' message was the coming of God's reign in mercy and judgement and the ingathering of the people of God at the end time. As God's agent, he did not make himself the direct object of his proclamation. Accordingly, during his ministry his identity was absorbed and defined by his mission, yet he seemed to be quite sure of who he was. Others tried to understand him by means of various titles and categories, but were not completely successful in this. The mystery of his person eluded them. He implicitly made himself the central figure in the eschatological drama he announced and inaugurated, for it was through his preaching and healings that the reign of God was being inaugurated. His hearers would be judged on the last day in accordance with their response to his call, and he spoke as if he himself would be the standard used. This suggests a unique status and role on his part.

It seems that Jesus enjoyed a deep experience of God whom he called Father (Abba). From his total abandonment to God and to God's will, sprang his teaching and activity. He taught his disciples to imitate him in his intimate relationship with God (Lk 11:2-4). This special connection that he had with his Father made a deep and lasting impression on the disciples and gave them an insight into Jesus' self-consciousness.

Jesus acted like the prophets of old, and more like the expected eschatological prophet. He referred to himself indirectly as a prophet in the context of his rejection in his hometown (cf Mk 6:4). If Jesus saw himself as the prophet of the end times anointed with the Spirit (Lk 4:16-21; cf Is 61:1-3),'then he would also be the messianic (anointed) prophet. Although there is no proof that Jesus directly referred to himself as the Messiah in the royal Davidic sense, yet he does not categorically reject it when Peter confessed him as the Messiah, but spoke of it with reserve. His disciples certainly seem to have thought of him as the Davidic Messiah in some way. Otherwise the post-Easter identification makes little sense (cf Rom 1:3-4). Jesus' actions and claims were without doubt understood in some royal messianic light, because his adversaries brought him to Pilate as King of the Jews.

It is possible that Jesus spoke of himself as Son or Son of God as a correlative of Father in a messianic or eschatological context. In the parable of the tenants (Mk 12:1-12), the son stands in line with the martyred prophets, and in Mt 11:27 Jesus claims mutual and exclusive knowledge between Father and Son as mediator of revelation. The title Son of Man is used in the gospels in three senses: in Jesus' earthly ministry as a modest circumlocution for self; in connection with his death and resurrection; in his future coming in judgement. We find this title in many different strata of the gospels on the lips of Jesus, and it is difficult to escape the conclusion that they go back to Jesus himself. Jesus was addressed as Lord with a whole range of meanings, from a polite form of address to being a mysterious person transcending all categories. The term Lord was developed by the post-Easter church as a term for worshipping the risen one. Jesus might well have been seen as a charismatic figure who could heal sickness, banish demons and control nature. Such a figure would inevitably have come into confrontation with the more institutional forms of Judaism represented by the Jerusalem hierarchy.

At the end of his ministry Jesus visited Jerusalem for the last time. It seems that some kind of happening, however modest, stands behind the accounts of his triumphal entry into Jerusalem as a symbolic claim to messianic status. The cleansing of the Temple would have staked a further claim to authority over the central cultic institution of the Jewish religion. This would have been seen as a prophetic gesture that the Temple was to be replaced and destroyed for a new and more perfect one. These actions would have provoked the priestly aristocracy who administered the Temple into apprehending Jesus. In view of the mounting opposition, which reached a crescendo during his last visit, he would have foreseen the possibility of a violent death in the capital city, as the rejected and martyred prophet, following John the Baptist. There are sayings in which Jesus speaks in a general way of his approaching death that cohere with his self-understanding.

Jesus celebrated a last supper with his disciples in the context of the Passover feast. He used the symbols of bread and wine to represent his coming death. His words on that occasion are recorded in four different versions. In spite of apparent failure, he said, God would vindicate him even beyond death and bring him and his followers to enjoy the eschatological banquet (cf Mk 14:25). After the supper, Jesus led his disciples to the Mount of Olives. While praying there he was arrested by an armed band sent by the High Priest, having already been betrayed by Judas, one of the Twelve. Jesus rejects armed resistance and the disciples flee in terror. It seems certain that some kind of trial followed, but because of divergent accounts in the gospels, it is difficult to be sure of the details. Jesus was arraigned before the High Priest following his arrest. Between his arrest and trial before Pilate, Jesus was held in custody by the Temple authorities. During the Jewish proceedings, Peter, who had followed, was confronted by the High Priest's servant, but he denied any relationship with Jesus.

Since Pilate would only be interested in political crimes, Jewish theological concerns would have been presented as Jesus being a false claimant to the Davidic throne. That is why he would have been tried and condemned as King of the Jews by Pilate and a notice referring to his crime would have been placed on the cross. Jesus was condemned to death by crucifixion after a preliminary scourging to hasten death. This left Jesus so weak that Simon had to be pressed into service to carry the crossbeam. Crucifixion took place outside the city walls at Golgotha where Jesus was nailed to the cross along with two robbers. Mockery and abuse filled the air as he hung on the cross. The words of Jesus as he was dying may be a later Christian interpretation in the light of the Old Testament. Some female disciples from Galilee witnessed his death which occurred before sundown, and the eve of the Passover that year coincided with the sabbath. Joseph interceded with Pilate, obtained the body for burial in a tomb he owned, and this was witnessed by the women.

CONCLUSION

By definition, the resurrection remains outside historical, empirical investigation. This does not mean that it is not real, but that resurrection transcends space and time as Jesus enters eternal life with God. But certain effects do belong to history: the empty tomb and the resurrection appearances. There were witnesses known by name who claimed that the risen Jesus appeared to them (1 Cor 15:5-8), including the disciples of the historical Jesus who had deserted him out of fear, but now were capable of launching a new movement. Some of them would even lay down their lives for the truth of their resurrection experiences. These are all historical facts. How one responds to these facts brings us into the realm of faith or unbelief.

CHAPTER SEVEN

Conclusion

We have seen that each of the evangelists has drawn their own portrait of Christ according to the traditions available to them, as well as conveying their own colourations in order to meet the needs of their audiences. Nevertheless, for all their differences, there is a profound unity between them. When we compare the four gospels, separated as they are in time and content, we discover that they are at the same level of faith.

DIVERSITY IN UNITY

We have assumed from the outset that Mark is the oldest gospel, that its author created an unique genre 'gospel', and had at his disposal certain traditions concerning Jesus of Nazareth which were regarded as reliable. From these he drew his faith picture of Christ which developed around the risen Lord. Mark presented Jesus, his words, his teaching, healings, exorcisms, miracles, epiphanies, and his confrontations with opponents, as well as his suffering and death. He also used certain names and titles for Jesus which he found in the tradition.

The sketch developed by Mark was familiar to Matthew and Luke, hence they adopted it and modified and adapted it. Matthew wanted to tell his story of Jesus in a new way, shaped in part from his contacts and conflicts with Judaism, but also from his view of the church as the sphere where the risen Jesus now continues his work. Matthew places emphasis on Jesus as the Son of David, the expected Messiah, who fulfils the Old Testament promises. He sought to present the person of Jesus and his teachings against the background of the Old Testament and Judaism. Mark had portrayed Jesus as teacher, but in

Matthew he becomes the teacher *par excellence*. Jesus does not abolish the Law, but fulfils it in a new way in keeping with the will of God. By his teaching, Jesus is the herald of the reign of God that is beginning to take root and grow in his new community, the church. Matthew's picture of Christ is extended by the addition of the infancy narratives and finds its completion in the Easter stories. The earthly Jesus has now become the risen Lord of his church.

Luke embarked on a more ambitious project by writing a two-volume work. In it he adopts a salvation history approach to the time of Jesus and beyond it to the beginning and growth of the church which resulted from the mission of Jesus. From a wealth of materials available to him, he offers further perspectives on the appearance and activity of Jesus. As a prophet sent by God in the power of the Spirit, he proclaimed the good news of God's graciousness especially to the 'nobodies' of society. He moves by way of suffering and death into God's glory. Jesus is Messiah, Lord and Saviour both of Jews and gentiles who, having ascended to God, sends the Holy Spirit to his church and becomes the guide to salvation. Luke presents an attractive picture of Jesus' humanity, his healing activity, his efforts on behalf of the poor and marginalised, his warm relationships with men and women alike, as well as being a man of prayer.

In the gospel of John, we find the synoptic Jesus in his healings, feeding the crowd, walking on the water and clashes with unbelieving Jews. Yet in John's gospel there is a considerable shift from the historical picture of Jesus in the synoptics to a christologically orientated presentation. Jesus is the incarnate *Logos*, the revealer of the Father who fulfils his work of revelation and salvation for human beings. He is the Son of Man who comes down from heaven and who, by way of the cross, ascends again to be glorified by the Father. This offers a more profound perspective that emphasises the divinity of Jesus, despite the fact that Jesus is also human and appeared historically on earth. In John, therefore, the portrait of Jesus Christ reaches its culmination.

UNITY IN DIVERSITY

In all the four gospels, Jesus' historical appearance among the Jewish people is presupposed and described in some detail. There is the conviction that he is the Messiah promised by the Old Testament prophets and expected at the end of time (cf Peter's confession in Mk 8:28-29). This idea is embraced by all the evangelists, with modifications or expansions based on each evangelist's viewpoint: in Matthew it is based on the full christo-logical confession of the early church (16:16); in Luke as one commissioned by God (9:20); in John as revealer and mediator of salvation who is close to God (6:69). It also comes to the fore in Jesus' public reply to the questioning of the High Priest (Mk 14:61-62 and par). In Matthew it is supported by many scriptural fulfilments (1:23, 2:6, etc.); in Luke the royal status of the Son of David is announced to Mary by the angel (1:32-33) and pro-claimed to the shepherds (2:10-11); in John Jesus is the Messiah whom Moses and the prophets announced (1:41, 45). Although in John he is also *Logos,* Revealer of God, he remains a historical human being, the expected Messiah of both Jews and Samaritans (cf 4:25-26). It is for this reason that the gospel was written (cf 20:31).

This Jewish Messiah, however, contrary to all expectations, is the one who gives his life for the salvation of human beings. His way to suffering and death is described at considerable length in all four gospels, even if variously interpreted in the post-Easter reflection of the community in order to gain some understand-ing of it. Jesus, the Messiah, became the kerygma of the early church that was taken over by the evangelists who also tried to understand this suffering Messiah in relation to God and human beings. In relation to God he is Son of God (cf Mk 1:1). For all four, the baptism is the occasion for the revelation of Jesus as Son of God. Already in Matthew he is God-with-us (1:23), the Son called out of Egypt (2:15). Later the disciples confess him: 'Truly you are the Son of God' (14:33) and Peter adds: 'Your are the Messiah, the Son of the living God' (16:16). The full identity for Jesus the Messiah includes his divine sonship. Luke also makes this clear in the angel's announcement to Mary that the child will be called 'Son of the Most High ... the Son of God' (1:32, 35). When he is questioned directly in the session before the Sanhedrin: 'Are you, then, the Son of God?' Jesus' answer is understood to be affirmative (22:67-70). In John, Nathaniel confesses: 'Rabbi, you are the Son of God! You are the King of Israel' (1:49), as does Martha: 'You are the Messiah, the Son of God, the one coming into the world' (11:27). The title Messiah is surpassed by Son of God which is an analogous expression borrowed from human experience. That Jesus is the unique Son of God was realised early on, was adopted by the synoptics, and reached it full expression in John (cf Jn 1:14, 18).

The beloved son sent by the owner in the parable of the wicked tenants (Mk 12:6) is the only begotten Son whom God sent out of love into the world (Jn 3:16). The Son who knows the Father as the Father knows him (Mt 11:27; Lk 10:22) is the Son nearest the Father's heart who has come to reveal him (Jn 1:18). The Son witnessed to by God in the baptismal and transfiguration scenes and acknowledged even by demons is the one who works closely with the Father (Jn 5:19), so that whoever sees him sees the Father also (Jn 14:9). The title Son of God spans from Mark's gospel to John's christology of the 'Son' in which the secret of the Son of God is fully revealed. The title accents his origin in God and his unique closeness to him.

Another conviction that is shared by all the evangelists is that Jesus is the healer and bringer of salvation. He heals the sick in body and soul and restores them to fellowship with God so that they can find peace again. They are rescued from demonic powers and freed from sin and guilt (cf Mk 1:41, 2:6, etc.). In Matthew the healings are understood to be works of the Messiah (11:2-6). In Luke, Jesus not only heals diseases of people in general, but also seeks out the sinners and the 'lost' (Lk 15). Jesus is the Saviour who releases captives, gives sight to the blind, frees the oppressed and proclaims the jubilee year (Lk 4:18-19). For John, Jesus brings eternal life for those who believe (Jn 3:16). In his Son, God bestows life and salvation (cf 5:21). Jesus is the bread of life, the light of the world, the resurrection and the life. In word and work Jesus is the giver of life that lasts forever, i.e. salvation. Already evident in the works and deeds of Jesus in the synoptics, John enhances their message of salvation.

The Son of God who appeared and worked on earth as Jesus of Nazareth reveals God in a new and challenging way. It is the transcendent God that Jesus proclaims, a God different from people's prior conception of him including those of the Jewish religious establishment. Jesus is portrayed in all the gospels as the messenger of God who inaugurates a reign of God that is different from popular expectation. He is the misunderstood one, a stranger even among his own people. Jesus' rebuke to Peter, who wanted to deflect him from the road of suffering, summarises this attitude: 'You are thinking not as God does, but as human beings do' (Mk 8:33; Mt 16:23). The inability of the Jewish leaders, and even of the disciples, to comprehend Jesus' message is expressed in Mark by means of the 'messianic secret'. In Matthew, it is Jesus' conflict with the Jewish authorities that leads to his death. It is his devotion to the poor and outcasts in Luke which is the reason for his suffering. While in John it is Jesus' announcement of God's truth and confrontation with the people that brings his ministry to an end. John expresses the people's misunderstanding and refusal to accept his message by means of dualistic language. Human beings are 'from below,' he is 'from above' (8:23). Only those who believe understand him, a small group in a darkened world that has turned away from God. The revelation of God through his only Son appearing on earth for the salvation of alienated human beings is a dominant theme of John's gospel. John's portrait of Christ in his relationship to God, humans and to a world estranged from God, is none other than the same Jesus we find in the synoptic gospels.

We have seen that the historical Jesus can only be inadequately recovered by modern scientific methods. The evangelists, on the other hand, give us a faith picture of Jesus Christ that encompasses both variety and a deeper unity, a portrait of Christ that has been accepted and pondered upon by Christians throughout the centuries. Is this portrait a myth, or does it give us a deeper appreciation of the person of Jesus? The evangelists do adopt traditions that date back to the historical Jesus and combine them with their faith in a crucified, resurrected and exalted Lord. All the evangelists are convinced that the stories of the life of Jesus reflect something that happened in time and place. Yet when we compare the gospels among themselves, we find tensions and even contradictory information. The efforts of historians to examine these traditions and trace them back to the historical Jesus is a worthwhile and justifiable exercise. Nevertheless, what can be achieved is only a general outline of the life of Jesus: his proclamation of the reign of God in word and deed, his gathering of disciples, his disagreements with Jewish opponents, his way to the cross. All the gospels are interpretations that go beyond the historically verifiable but formed part of the tradition available to the evangelists.

The evangelists set out from a certain vantage point regarding the person of Jesus and within that framework they sought to arrange the concrete traditions of Jesus' words and deeds. These are all developed by each evangelist on the basis of his own christology. The evangelists take for granted the historical foundation of Jesus' deeds, sayings, disputes and disagreements with contemporaries. The evangelists, therefore, did not put together their portrait of Jesus from individual traditions in some sort of mosaic-like fashion. Rather they began with an overall faith picture of his person and incorporated individual stories and episodes into it. The gospels reveal rather the character of Jesus, which cannot be fully fathomed, but only revealed as a mystery and grasped in faith. The mystery of his person, which Mark has already underlined in his motif of the messianic secret, cannot be grasped by a consideration based only on the outward human person of Jesus. It must include that hidden part of his person, i.e. his rootedness in God. The evangelists attempt to express this aspect by means of various titles. Without anchoring it in God, the person of Jesus remains elusive and incomprehensible. Each evangelist in his own way reveals the mystery of the person of Jesus that reaches its culmination in John. The historical dimension, while not totally available to modern historical methods, is still palpable to anyone who reads the gospels. The faith portrait of Jesus Christ, then, is not a product of dreams or fantasies.

The gospel in its fourfold form stretches over several decades to the end of the first century and testifies to the good news brought by Jesus Christ who now becomes the good news himself in the post-Easter period. Four gospels, no more, no less, alone guarantee the apostolic traditions that go back to Jesus. The four canonical gospels offer the most important and lasting elements of the revelation brought by Jesus Christ and offer a glimpse of his person both in his historical existence and in his meta-historical significance.

Epilogue

Despite the real differences between the gospels and their portraits of Christ, it is one and the same Jesus who demonstrates a lifestyle that embraces obedience to God, his Father, and self-giving for the sake of others. He invites those who follow him to embrace that same lifestyle so that their lives can be progressively transformed into his. It is the character of Jesus of Nazareth, as a human person and the manner of his living, that remains normative for Christians. The pattern of faithful adherence to God and of faithful service, even to the point of death, for all becomes capable of realisation in the lives of believers through the power of the Spirit. That is the reason why the passion narratives occupy such a prominent place in all the four gospels, and why the cross stands as the central symbol of Christian discipleship. A prayerful meditation on the gospel narratives can be a personal enrichment for every Christian and should be part of what it means to belong to the Christian community that confesses Jesus as Lord and Saviour.

The manner in which Jesus is portrayed in the four gospels also corresponds with the many facets of Christian discipleship. In Mark's focus on the personhood of Jesus, Christians are reminded that their commitment is first and foremost to a person. The mystery of a suffering Messiah demands faithfulness and fidelity in the face of suffering and death. Matthew reveals that Christians' commitment to the person of Jesus is lived out within the community of believers that confesses him as Lord. Under the authority which he himself established, they are guided in how to daily live the Christian life. Luke-Acts spells out Christians' obligation to bear witness to those outside the community. As Jesus' prophetic successors, they proclaim the good news with conviction to the world. Finally, John recalls for Christians the truth that living and witnessing are effective only on condition that they remain united with Jesus as branches of the vine, while the Spirit leads them into the truth that is lived out in loving service of one another. In the four gospels then, the christological, ecclesiological, missionary, and contemplative dimensions of the Christian vocation are fully delineated and clearly set forth.

The gospels are best appreciated within the canon of sacred scripture and within the church's living tradition that interprets them. They are human compositions and so are naturally incomplete, yet the church professes that they are inspired by the Spirit, and so are true witnesses to the person of Jesus. They are not simple reports of facts, nor are they caricatures of his person; they are portraits resulting from decades of reflection and the appropriation of earlier traditions. The church accepts these four gospels as articulations of the character and ministry of a person who is still richer and more mysterious than human beings can ever comprehend or fathom.

FOR FURTHER READING

Best, E., *Mark: The Gospel as Story*, Edinburgh: T & T Clark, 1983

Brown, R. E., *An Introduction to New Testament Christology*, New York: Paulist Press, 1994

— *An Introduction to the New Testament*, New York: Doubleday, 1997

Culpepper, R. A., *The Gospel and Letters of John*, Nashville: Abingdon Press, 1998

Dunn, J. D. G., *Christology in the Making*, Second Edition, London: SCM Press, 1989

Fitzmyer, J. A., *A Christological Catechism*, New York: Paulist Press, 1991

Harrington, D.J., *Matthew*, Sacra Pagina, Collegeville: Liturgical Press, 1991

Harrington, W., *Mark*, Dublin: Veritas, 1980

Johnson, L. T., *Luke*, Sacra Pagina, Collegeville: Liturgical Press, 1991

— *Acts of the Apostles*, Sacra Pagina, Collegeville: Liturgical Press, 1992

— *The Real Jesus*, San Francisco: HarperCollins, 1996

— *Living Jesus*, San Francisco: HarperCollins, 1999

— *The Writings of the New Testament*, Second Edition, London: SCM, 1999

Matera, F. J., *New Testament Christology*, Louisville, Ky: Westminster John Knox, 1999

Meier, J. P.; *Matthew*, Dublin: Veritas, 1980

— *A Marginal Jew: Rethinking the Historical Jesus*, 2 vols, New York: Doubleday, 1991, 1994

— 'Jesus,' *The New Jerome Biblical Commentary* (R. E. Brown, J. A. Fitzmeyer, R. E. Murphy, eds), London: Chapman, 1990, pp 1316-28

Moloney, F. J., *John*, Sacra Pagina, Collegeville: Liturgical Press, 1998

Rhoads, D., Dewey, J., Michie, D., *Mark as Story: An Introduction to the Narrative of a Gospel*, Second Edition, Minneapolis: Fortress Press, 1999

Schnackenburg, R., *Jesus in the Gospels: A Biblical Christology*, Westminster: John Knox, 1995

Senior, D., *Matthew*, Nashville: Abingdon Press, 1998

Tannehill, R. C., *Luke*, Nashville: Abingdon Press, 1996

Van Iersel, Bas, *Reading Mark*, Edinburgh: T &T Clark, 1989

Witherington, B. III, *The Many Faces of Christ*, New York: Crossroad, 1998